KV-571-760

Contents

List of Tables   vi

List of Figures   viii

Acknowledgements   ix

Glossary   x

1. Shipping and Port Development in Southeast Asia: 1
    An Overview

2. Port Development Policies in Southeast Asia: 24
    A Comparative Analysis

3. Hub Ports   52

4. Forecast of Container Volumes and Patterns of   75
    Transhipment

5. The Seaport Model   91

6. Conclusion   102

Index   105

The Authors   111

List of Tables

Table 1.1 World container traffic, 1990–97   4

Table 1.2 General and container ships of   6
Asia–Pacific countries, December 1996

Table 1.3 Ten largest container ports in Asia, 1990–98   8

Table 1.4 Large and significant Asian ports, 1998   10

Table 1.5 Technological improvement in container ships   11

Table 1.6 Shipping alliances, 1998   15

Table 1.7 Container trade on major Asian routes   19

Table 2.1 Changes in ship size   28

Table 2.2 Proportion of transhipments to total   33
throughput in major ports, 1996

Table 2.3 Containers handled at Port Klang, 1995–2000   40

Table 3.1 Handling charges per container, 1999   70

Table 4.1 Forecast world container port demand to 2012   77

90 0636074 X

SOUTHEAST ASIAN REGIONAL PORT DEVELOPMENT

WITHDRAWN
FROM
UNIVERSITY OF PLYMOUTH
LIBRARY SERVICES

The **Institute of Southeast Asian Studies (ISEAS)** was established as an autonomous organization in 1968. It is a regional research centre for scholars and other specialists concerned with modern Southeast Asia, particularly the many-faceted problems of stability and security, economic development, and political and social change.

The Institute's research programmes are the Regional Economic Studies (RES, including ASEAN and APEC), Regional Strategic and Political Studies (RSPS), and Regional Social and Cultural Studies (RSCS).

The Institute is governed by a twenty-two-member Board of Trustees comprising nominees from the Singapore Government, the National University of Singapore, the various Chambers of Commerce, and professional and civic organizations. An Executive Committee oversees day-to-day operations; it is chaired by the Director, the Institute's chief academic and administrative officer.

SOUTHEAST ASIAN REGIONAL PORT DEVELOPMENT
A Comparative Analysis

Chia Lin Sien
Mark Goh
Jose Tongzon

INSTITUTE OF SOUTHEAST ASIAN STUDIES
SINGAPORE

University of Plymouth
Library

Item No 900636074X

Shelfmark

First published in Singapore in 2003 by
Institute of Southeast Asian Studies
30 Heng Mui Keng Terrace
Pasir Panjang
Singapore 119614

E-mail: publish@iseas.edu.sg
Website: http://bookshop.iseas.edu.sg

All rights reserved. No part of this publication may be reproduced, stored in a retrieval system, or transmitted in any form or by any means, electronic, mechanical, photocopying, recording or otherwise, without the prior permission of the Institute of Southeast Asian Studies.

© 2003 Institute of Southeast Asian Studies, Singapore.

The responsibility for facts and opinions in this publication rests exclusively with the authors and their interpretations do not necessarily reflect the views or the policy of the Institute or its supporters.

ISEAS Library Cataloguing-in-Publication Data

Chia, Lin Sien
Southeast Asian regional port development : a comparative analysis/
Chia Lin Sien, Mark Goh, Jose Tongzon.
    1. Harbours — Asia, Southeastern.
    2. Harbours — Government policy — Asia, Southeastern.
    I. Goh, Mark.
    II. Tongzon, Jose.
    III. Title.
HE559 A9C53   2003   sls2002023112

ISBN 981-230-183-6

The photograph of a container ship on the front cover was obtained from Corbis Corporation.

Typeset by International Typesetters Pte Ltd.
Printed in Singapore by Primepak Services.

Table 4.2   Forecast East Asian container port demand by region   81

Table 4.3   Forecast global transhipment by region   84

Table 4.4   Forecast regional share of global transhipment market   86

Table 4.5   Forecast transhipment incidence by region   87

Table 5.1   List of ports   92

Table 5.2   Optimal route from Mumbai to Tokyo using different criteria   95

Table 5.3   Optimal routing based on transit times and costs   98

List of Figures

Figure 1.1 World container traffic, 1982–98   4

Figure 1.2 Container ships by country, number of ships   6
and gross tonnage, 1999

Figure 1.3 Total merchant shipping fleet by country,   7
number of ships and gross tonnage, 1999

Figure 3.1 Growth rate of containers handled   71

Figure 3.2 Crane productivity   72

Figure 4.1 Total world port volumes 1983–98   76

Figure 5.1 Optimal route from Mumbai to Tokyo via   97
Port Klang based purely on cost criteria

Figure 5.2 Optimal route from Mumbai to Tokyo via   97
Singapore based on 30 : 70 cost–time ratio

Figure 5.3 Optimal route from Manila to Shanghai   99
based on cost only

Figure 5.4 Optimal route from Manila to Shanghai   100
based on transit time only

Figure 5.5 Optimal route from Manila to Shanghai   100
based on service frequency

Acknowledgements

It is impossible to list all the individuals who have contributed ideas and information to this book. We are grateful to all parties who have allowed us to study the various ports, visited or otherwise; to those in support organizations and government related agencies who freely share their knowledge; and to all individuals who knowingly or unknowingly provided helpful insights. Many thanks too to the Institute of Southeast Asian Studies in Singapore, which graciously supported the funding for this research. Special thanks also to those at the Institute for housing the researchers and assisting them in more ways than one.

Glossary

Terms

ALS	Approved Shipping Enterprise Scheme
APEC	Asia-Pacific Economic Cooperation
dwt	dead weight tonnes
EDI	electronic data interchange
FCL	full container loads
GATT	General Agreement on Trade and Tariffs
gt	gross tonnes
HIT	Hong Kong International Terminal
IAPH	International Association of Ports and Harbors
IMO	International Maritime Organization
IT	information technology
ITPMIS	integrated terminal and port management information systems
JIT	just-in-time
KCM	Key Customer Manager; person who looks after individual customer needs
KCT	Klang Container Terminal
KPA	Klang Port Authority
LCL	less than container load
LCP	Laem Chabang Port
MISC	Malaysian International Shipping Corporation
MLO	main shipping-line operator
MPA	Maritime and Port Authority (Singapore)
mt	metric tonnes
NOL	Neptune Orient Lines (Singapore)

OECD	Organization for Economic Cooperation and Development
PAT	Port of Thailand Authority
PIL	Pacific International Lines (Singapore)
PPA	Philippine Ports Authority
PSA	Port of Singapore Authority
RCL	Regional Container Line (Thailand)
TEUs	twenty-foot container equivalent units
THC	terminal handling charges
TPK Koja	Tanjung Priok Koja Container Terminal
ULCC	ultra large crude carrier
UNCTAD	United Nations Conference on Trade and Development
USD/TEU	U.S. dollars per twenty-foot container
VLCC	very large crude carrier
WTO	World Trade Organization

1

Shipping and Port Development in Southeast Asia: An Overview

The countries of Southeast Asia depend heavily on marine transport and benefit greatly from the participation of international trade and shipping. Although Southeast Asia does not generate large volumes of bulk cargo such as oil, iron ore, and grain, rapid industrial development in the core countries of the region (Thailand, Malaysia, Singapore, Indonesia and the Philippines) since the 1970s has produced large volumes of containerizable cargo. Early growth in containerization was due to the conversion of general cargo into boxed cargo. Subsequent growth has been due largely to increases in both the imports and exports of containerized cargo comprising a wide range of manufactured goods. Several of the container ports in the region are among the top twenty in the world. Singapore and Hong Kong (not considered as part of Southeast Asia proper) vie with each other as the world's top ranked ports.

Apart from landlocked Laos, all Southeast Asian states rightly consider themselves as maritime nations. The importance given to the promotion of shipping in a maritime nation is perhaps best exemplified by Malaysia. The country's trade grew phenomenally from RM60 billion (US$24 billion) in 1989 to RM258 billion in 1993, a fourfold increase. Of this total, some 97 per cent of the trade is seaborne. However, although Malaysia possesses a sizeable merchant shipping fleet, 85 per cent of its trade is transported by foreign vessels (the remainder is carried on Malaysian-registered vessels). Malaysia hence paid RM309 million in 1972, RM4.52 billion in 1992 and over RM6 billion in 1994 for foreign shipping services. The net payment for freight and insurance was RM4.8 billion in 1991 (Hamzah 1995). Malaysia, like some other Southeast Asian states, has also invested heavily in port infrastructure and has made serious attempts at improving the nation's port services in order to attract foreign vessels to call at its ports. One objective is to transform the country's premier port, Port Klang, into a hub port. Determined efforts have also gone into developing Pasir Gudang in Johor, located near to the Port of Singapore, in order to carry the country's own cargo. In addition, a new port, the Port of Tanjung Pelepas, was created at the western end of the Johor Straits, across from Singapore, to capture cargo and to attract vessels away from Singapore (see Chapter 2). The rapid development of both Malaysia's shipping and sea ports epitomises the competitiveness and vibrancy of the region. Later chapters in this book will explore this phenomenon and similar developments elsewhere in the region.

In the case of Singapore, it has been estimated that in 1999 the port and its related industries contributed 4.8 per cent of the country's GDP, or almost US$3.7 billion. The port and related industries employed 55,392 workers or about 3.4 per cent of the total workforce. Indeed, one observer commented that "the port is Singapore, and Singapore is the port" and that maritime operations serve as the nation's heritage and identity (Embassy of the United States of America 1997). In effect, shipping and port operations are so closely related to trade, forming a large part of the country's manufacturing industry, that they constitute the economic lifeline of the country.

Growth of containerized cargo

Worldwide, the total amount of cargo traded between countries yearly is about 5.5 billion metric tonnes (mt), valued at some

US$4,000 billion, with four-fifths of the goods accounted for by seaborne trade (*Containerisation International Yearbook* 1997). Of these, 750 million mt are general cargo (including containerized cargo), accounting for about 50 per cent of the value of goods carried, largely because this cargo includes semi-manufactured and finished products that have high value per tonne (APEC 1996). The volume of this general cargo is growing yearly. It is predicted that by the year 2005, seaborne cargo will total 5,350 million mt, of which general cargo will account for 960 million mt or 18 per cent of the total (Thomas 1996; *Containerisation International Yearbook* 1997).

Of the 750 million mt a year of seaborne general cargo, about 350 million mt (or 47 per cent of the total) are carried in containers. This is only about 8 per cent of the total seaborne trade by weight, but it represents over 40 per cent by value, which indicates its importance. However, this 350 million mt figure conceals considerable differences among the many trade routes. About 80 per cent of general cargo movement between the developed market economies and the newly industrializing economies is now containerized. By the year 2005, it is predicted that total ship-borne general cargo will reach 960 million mt and the proportion (by weight) of general cargo carried in containers will rise to 54 per cent or 520 million mt (APEC 1995; Drewry 1998).

Compared with the rate of growth of air cargo, which has been growing in excess of 5 per cent annually for the past ten years, the growth of cargo carried by ships has registered an average of just 2 per cent per year worldwide (World Bank 1996). However, maritime transport is still an expanding activity; in 1997 it registered its twelfth consecutive year of growth with a volume of 5,074 billion mt. Figure 1.1 shows the rapid growth of container cargo for the period 1982–1998. The number of containers moved over the period increased from 42.8 million TEUs (twenty-foot equivalent units) in 1992 to 171.5 million TEUs in 1998, a fourfold increase over the period. As a proportion of general cargo trade, containerized cargo increased from 37 per cent in 1990 to 48 per cent in 1995 and 54 per cent in 1999.[1] Table 1.1 shows the change in world container traffic by region between 1990 and 1997. Over this period, the average annual

TABLE 1.1

World Container Traffic, 1990–97

(million TEUs)

Region	1990	Per cent share	1997	Per cent share	Per cent per annum[a] increase
North America	16.7	19.5	24.5	14.4	5.6
Western Europe	22.4	26.2	38.6	22.7	4.9
Asia	37.9	44.3	81.7	48.1	12.8
Far East	23.0	26.9	47.8	28.1	11.0
Southeast Asia	9.6	11.2	25.6	15.0	15.0
Middle East	3.5	4.1	8.0	4.7	12.5
South Asia	1.8	2.1	4.3	4.3	13.2
South America	4.8	5.6	11.5	6.8	13.3
Africa	1.8	2.1	3.2	2.0	8.9
East Europe	0.4	0.5	0.6	0.38	4.8
Oceania	2.1	2.5	2.4	1.5	4.2
Others	2.1	2.5	2.5	1.6	8.7
World total	**85.6**	**6.4**	**169.9**	**5.8**	**8.5**

Source: *Containerisation International Yearbook* (1996); Drewry (1998).

FIGURE 1.1

World Container Traffic, 1982–98

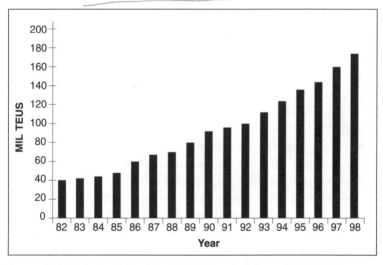

Source: *Containerisation International Yearbook*, various issues (1985–2000).

rate of increase of traffic grew by 8.5 per cent for the world as a whole. For Asia, the volume grew from 37.9 million TEUs in 1990 to 81.7 million TEUs in 1997, averaging a growth rate of 12.8 per cent per annum, just lower than the 13.3 per cent per year growth experienced in South America. Within the region, Southeast Asia registered a growth rate of 15 per cent per year, higher than any other region; and, significantly, South Asia grew by an average of 13.2 per cent per year. It is expected that by 2005, over 50 per cent of all container movements will be through Asian ports, while container traffic in Europe is expected to grow by 20 per cent, in North America by 30 per cent, and in Asia by as much as 60 per cent (*Containerisation International Yearbook* 1996; APEC 1996).

Shipping fleets

There are giants and minnows among Asian countries by way of shipping fleet size. By the end 1999, Japan, the world's second largest ship-owning country, had 70.6 million gt (gross tonnes), well above the rest in Asia. The next group of countries possessing between 10 and 30 million gt are China, Hong Kong SAR, South Korea, Taiwan and Singapore. China, with 27 million gt, acquired many second-hand ships from the 1970s onwards, but since the 1990s it has been acquiring modern ships with an average age of 17 years, putting the nation's fleet in terms of age just behind that of Japan (11 years), Singapore (13 years), and Hong Kong (14 years).

In terms of beneficially-owned ships, Japan, with 2,915 vessels totalling 118.4 million dwt (dead weight tonnes), is second after Greece (end 1996 figures). China featured well, with 1,972 ships totalling 36.3 million dwt; it ranked 5th in the world, followed by Hong Kong SAR (ranking), South Korea (ranking) and Taiwan (ranking). Several countries in Southeast Asia ranked among the world's top 30 ship-owning states (see Table 1.2). Singapore was ranked 14th, Philippines 27th, Indonesia and Thailand 29th and 30th respectively, while Malaysia was ranked 31st (UNCTAD 1997). Figures 1.2 and 1.3 show graphically the sizes of nationally-registered container

TABLE 1.2

General and Container Ships of Asia–Pacific Countries, December 1996

Country	General cargo (gt)	Container ships (gt)
Australia	115,247	77,162
China	5,431,260	1,388,957
Hong Kong SAR	759,447	865,588
Taiwan	n/a	n/a
Japan	2,380,491	1,097,376
South Korea	935,561	1,637,761
India	576,561	84,345
Sri Lanka	132,922	0
Brunei	2,723	0
Cambodia	0	0
Indonesia	1,231,195	60,623
Laos	0	0
Malaysia	693,613	415,532
Myanmar	232,719	24,415
Philippines	1,830,389	166,128
Singapore	2,245,811	2,294,879
Thailand	967,301	78,178
Vietnam	469,864	0
World total	**99,377,595**	**43,290,409**

Source: UNCTAD (1997), Annex III(a).

FIGURE 1.2

Container Ships by Country, Number of Ships and Gross Tonnage, 1999

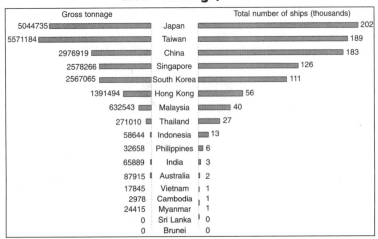

Source: UNCTAD (1997), Annex III(a).

FIGURE 1.3
Total Merchant Shipping Fleet by Country, Number of Ships and Gross Tonnage, 1999

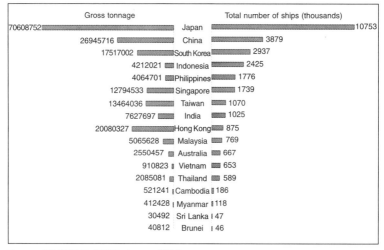

Source: UNCTAD (1997), Annex III(a).

ships and total fleet sizes, respectively, of Asian countries for the year 1999.

The five core countries of Southeast Asia have all vigorously promoted marine transport by various means, such as setting up shipping registries, establishing state-owned shipping lines, adopting policies that favour national shipping companies, signing bilateral shipping agreements and adopting cabotage regulations that restrict the carriage of cargo among national ports to ships registered in the country concerned (Chia and Lim 1981; Brooks 1985; Trace and Chia 1988).

Container ports

As this book is concerned with container liner shipping, this and subsequent sections will focus primarily on this aspect of shipping and ports. As port competition extends well beyond the region itself, discussion will include major ports in the neighbouring area, primarily those in East Asia. Asia's container

TABLE 1.3
Ten Largest Container Ports in Asia, 1990–98

Rank	1990	TEUs	1995	TEUs	1997	TEUs	1998	TEUs
1	Singapore	5,223,500	Hong Kong	12,549,746	Hong Kong	14,567,231	Singapore	15,100,000
2	Hong Kong	5,100,637	Singapore	10,800,300	Singapore	14,135,300	Hong Kong	14,582,000
3	Kaohsiung	3,494,631	Kaohsiung	5,232,000	Kaohsiung	5,693,339	Kaohsiung	6,271,053
4	Kobe	2,595,940	Busan	4,502,596	Busan	5,233,880	Busan	5,945,614
5	Busan	2,348,475	Yokohama	2,756,811	Shanghai	2,520,000	Shanghai	3,066,000
6	Keelung	1,807,271	Tokyo	2,177,407	Yokohama	2,347,635	Manila	2,690,000
7	Yokohama	1,647,891	Keelung	2,169,893	Tokyo	2,322,000	Tokyo	2,168,543
8	Tokyo	1,555,140	Manila	1,687,743	Manila	2,121,074	Tanjung Priok	2,130,979
9	Bangkok	1,018,290	Shanghai	1,527,000	Tanjung Priok	2,091,402	Yokohama	2,091,420
10	Manila	1,014,396	Nagoya	1,477,359	Kobe	1,944,147	Kobe	1,900,737

Source: *Containerisation International Yearbook*, various issues (1992–2000).

ports, including those in Southeast Asia, rank highly among world ports, as is shown in Table 1.3. Asian ports have shown remarkable growth performance since the 1980s, especially in the late 1980s, continuing to grow for most of the 1990s until the financial crisis in mid 1997. As mentioned earlier, Hong Kong and Singapore vie for pole position while Kaohsiung, with about less than half of the throughput (from 1997) of that of the top two ports, has held the third position consistently. The earthquake in January 1995 that severely damaged Kobe caused the port[2] to disappear from the top ten container ports in 1995. However, the port was completely rebuilt and it re-emerged in tenth position in 1998. The Korean port of Busan has held fourth position since 1995. Ports worth noting include Shanghai, Manila and Tanjung Priok, which improved their ranking over the second half of the 1990s. This was due to investments made to augment container-port infrastructure, changes in shipping patterns and increased trade involving containerized cargo during this period.

Table 1.4 lists major and significant ports in the Asian region. In China, apart from Hong Kong, four ports (Shanghai, Dalian, Qingdao and Tianjin) are in the million TEU bracket (1998 figures). The port of Colombo in Sri Lanka is especially noteworthy, as it handled 1.7 million TEUs in 1998 and can be considered as the premier port on the Indian subcontinent. Within Southeast Asia, the privatized South Harbour in Manila handled 2.7 million TEUs and is shaping up to become a major container port within the region, being in strong position to make further gains in the future. In Thailand, the government's decision to establish in the early 1990s the Port of Laem Chabang on the southeastern coast was intended to provide new capacity to meet unfulfilled demand from the Port of Bangkok. In 1998, the private container operators of Laem Chabang handled 1.6 million TEUs, comparing favourably with Bangkok's 1.1 million TEUs (Table 1.4). The strategy of developing a deep-sea container port, as part of the country's plan to develop the southeastern seaboard as an industrial zone to replace the shallow, constricted and hazardous port in Bangkok, has clearly shown positive results.

TABLE 1.4

Large and Significant Asian Ports, 1998

Country	Port	TEUs	Rank
China	Hong Kong	14,582,000	2
	Shanghai	3,066,000	10
	Qingdao	1,214,000	33
	Yantian	1,038,074	40
	Tianjin	1,018,000	41
India	Jawaharlal Nehru	669,080	64
	Mumbai	509,310	75
	Channai	320,000	104
Japan	Tokyo	2,168,543	15
	Yokohama	2,091,420	18
	Kobe	1,900,737	20
South Korea	Busan	5,945,614	5
Sri Lanka	Colombo	1,714,077	24
Taiwan	Kaohsiung	6,271,053	3
	Keelung	1,191,793	34
	Taichung	880,239	48
✓ Indonesia	Tanjung Priok	2,130,979	16
	Ujung Pandang	102,415	175
✓ Malaysia	Port Klang	1,820,018	22
	Penang	509,169	76
	Johor	460,000	77
✓ Philippines	Manila	2,690,000	12
	Cebu	333,283	99
	Davao	143,433	152
✓ Singapore	PSA	15,100,000	1
✓ Thailand	Laem Chabang	1, 559,112	26
	Bangkok	1,079,794	38

Source: *Containerisation International Yearbook* (2000).

Adoption of advanced technology and information technology

The need for increased shipping activities to cope with the rapid rise in commodity trade has generated considerable pressure on the operating environment of major sea ports and their allied services. The response to this has been to adopt new and improved technology in both the vessels and the landside operation of ports and land-transport facilities. It is important to note too that there have been shifts in customer preferences, greater rivalry and competition among ports, and changes in the physical and business relationships between various segments within the maritime transport industry as well as with other transport modes. Table 1.5 shows the continuing technical development in container ships since the 1960s. The increasing size and sophistication of ships and port facilities require heavy capital investment that is often beyond the means of developing countries. The start of the 1980s saw the emergence of global alliances, mergers and acquisitions that duplicated the experience of the airline industry. Consequently, the emphasis of shipping from the 1960s to the late 1980s was on containerization and through-transport systems. Containerization enabled the operation of "multi-modalism" and had the effect of sharply raising productivity in both ocean and land transportation.

The structural changes in shipping services have had a profound effect on the operation of seaports and terminals. Currently, container ships of 3,500 TEUs in size and the post-Panamax designs are the fastest growing segment. However, increasingly, very large vessels of 6,000 TEUs and larger are being deployed. Vessels of 8,000 TEUs are being envisaged and forecasts of 12,000 TEU vessels have even been made. More and larger quay cranes and terminal-handling facilities with greater sophistication are needed to cater to the new generation of

TABLE 1.5

Technological Improvement in Container Ships

	1960s	1970s	1980s	1984+	1992+	1996+	2000+
Length (m)	190	210	210–290	270–300	290–320	305–310	355–360
Width (m)	27	27	32	37–41	38–47	38–40	38–40
Draught (m)	9	10	11.5	13–14	13–14	13.5–14	15
Speed (kph)	16	23	23	24–24.8	25	25	NA
Capacity (TEU)	1,000	2,000	3,000	4,000+	4,900+	6,000	6,600

Source: Kang and Findlay (1998).

cellular vessels. The new generation of ports and harbours are required to have the following facilities:

1. Gantry cranes with a span width of 17 containers
2. Habour channels that can accommodate ships with 50 ft (15.4 m) drafts
3. Terminals capable of handling large numbers of containers efficiently
4. Rail and intermodal infrastructure must expand to handle growing volumes of cargo (Olsen 1999).

Automation and computerization to improve cargo-handling performance and efficiency are now supporting mechanization. The integration of maritime and inland transport services is having a significant impact on container flow patterns, and is changing transport systems as well as the traditional role of organizations in the maritime industry. Containerization has raised efficiency to enable low-cost products such as pulp and paper to move (Olsen 1999). Refrigerated containers have long been utilized to create new markets for a wide range of perishable products. Real-time information is now made available to shippers to enable them to track their cargo, so that they can make decisions with greater certainty. Such technical innovations and improvements have changed the relationship between port authorities, terminal operators, freight forwarders, shipping lines and agencies, customs brokers, warehousing and logistics companies in the maritime transport industry. Alliances among different segments of the industry share information and enter into partnerships in carrying and handling goods. These developments provide a platform for the liberalization of maritime transport and service, which in turn has eased access across national (and regional) borders to take advantage of the capability of a highly integrated industry.

Since the 1980s, new operating practices and procedures have been introduced. The high volume and speed of container movements require comprehensive and reliable control systems. Greater emphasis is placed on operational planning in terminals because of the sheer speed of the operation and the enormous penalties that result from any delays that may affect the very large, expensive container vessels while in port. Much of this work is presently carried out by advanced computer technologies and there have been significant advances in the development of systems to monitor and control container movements, including the introduction of electronic data interchange (EDI) systems.

Customs formalities and documentation procedures have had to be revised, and the introduction of computerization and EDI have fundamentally altered the way in which information is relayed and have greatly improved communications in the industry. The wider role of sea–land transport in facilitating the globalization trend, and the significant impact of IT in the integration of the transportation chain to meet the real-time delivery requirements of multinational corporations, is the primary concern of the IT revolution in the shipping industry.

Related to this is the development of major hub ports and the shift towards multimodalism and, inevitably, towards logistics operations and the increasing use of IT. The employment of IT in the port and shipping community has radically altered ocean transportation through changing trading patterns, ship routing and itineraries, ship design and size, cargo handling equipment and operations, inland transport and freight terminals, commercial practices and customs procedures (Chia et al. 1999).

Alliances, mergers and acquisitions

The maritime transport services have followed global trends towards privatization, alliances and acquisitions. Privatization of state-owned shipping companies includes the Australian National Lines, the Malaysian International Shipping Corporation (MISC) and Singapore's Neptune Orient Lines (NOL). In 1996, the Port of Singapore Authority[3] corporatized its commercial arm, PSA Corporation, in order to operate flexibly in a highly competitive environment. Alliances of major shipping lines include the Maersk (Denmark)-Sealand (USA) arrangement (200 container vessels), the Global Alliance comprising American President Lines (USA), Mitsui OSK (Japan), Orient Overseas Container Lines (Hong Kong), Nedlloyd (Netherlands) and Malaysian International Shipping Company, the Grand Alliance that includes Hapag Lloyd

(Germany), NOL (Singapore), NYK (Japan) and P&O (UK) and, finally, the alliance between Hanjin (Korea), DSR-Senator (Germany), Cho Yang (South Korea) and United Arab Shipping Company (Arab multinational).

Alliances within the framework of shipping conferences that was previously dedicated to specific routes, such as Scandutch or Trio between Europe and the Far-East or ACL on the Atlantic, have become global. This implies worldwide cooperation between the shipping lines concerned. Buyouts or takeovers of transnationals include the acquisition of APL by NOL, of DSR-Senator Line (Germany) by Hanjin, acquisition of Blue Star by P&O and Nedlloyd, or the merger between P&O and Nedlloyd. In 1999, Maersk acquired South Africa Marine Line and bought the largest US container carrier, Sealand. The process of consolidation into a handful of mega-carriers is the result of many failures and successes, mergers and acquisitions affecting hundreds of local and regional companies. Table 1.6 shows the estimated capacity of major global alliances in container shipping (1998 figures). It is interesting to note that among the names of companies listed in the table, Asian shipping lines feature prominently, although only two Southeast Asian lines, Malaysia's MISC and Singapore's NOL, are represented among the élite group of liner shipping companies.

The information contained in the Table 1.6 has already been altered by more recent developments. A survey by Alphaliner for the year ending 1 January 2001 (Urquhart 2001) reports that the top 25 carriers make up half of global container-ship capacity while the top 100 carriers account for about 91 per cent of a total of 5.2 million TEUs. For individual shipping groups, the largest is AP Moller, with its subsidiaries Maersk-Sealand and Safmarine accounting for nearly a 12 per cent gain in capacity, or 74,000 TEUs, over the previous year. The group has 31 ships totalling some 130,902 TEUs, on order and is therefore set to expand further. During the year 2000, P&O Nedlloyd overtook Evergreen Group for the second spot. It experienced an increase of 22.4 per cent capacity to reach 343,000 TEUs. On order are 21 vessels totalling 84,032 TEUs. The Taiwanese Evergreen Group's fleet at 325,000 TEUs grew slightly by 2.4 per cent over the year and is in third

TABLE 1.6
Shipping Alliances, 1998

Alliance	Members	Vessels (No.)	Fleet capacity (TEUs)
Grand	Hapag-Lloyd	23	73,372
	MISC	26	58,299
	NYK	68	128,154
	OOCL	30	85,940
	P&O Nedlloyd	106	221,531
New World	Hyundai	36	112,985
	Mitsui-OSK	62	115,763
	NOL/APL	74	165,582
United	Hanjin/DRS Senator	62	174,526
	Cho Yang	30	55,882
	UASC	33	71,592
Maersk/Sealand	Maersk	106	232,257
	Sealand	95	215,114
K-Line/Yangming/	K-Line	45	84,198
Cosco	Yangming	42	96,145
	Cosco	139	201,593
Evergreen/Uniglory Marine Corp		108	228,248
Total		**1,085**	**2,321,154**

Source: Seet-Cheng (1998).

position. The group had acquired an Italian company, Lloyd Triestino, that operates 20 ships totalling 77,000 TEUs. APL, owned by Singapore's NOL, grew by 8 per cent to reach 224,000 TEUs. APL has on order 16 vessels totalling 69,000 TEUs. The three large Korean operators remain within the top 25 shipping lines, with Hanjin and its erstwhile German line, Senator, increasing by 5.5 per cent to 258,023 TEUs. Hyundai Merchant Marine increased by 3.7 per cent while Cho Yang Line reduced its capacity by 8 per cent.

Interestingly, in the same report, the Singapore-registered Pacific International Lines (PIL) was ranked in 24th position, recording a strong 21 per cent growth in capacity to a total of 73,000 TEU. Also, the Thai-based Regional Container Line (RCL), which operates mainly out of Singapore, also experienced a 25 per cent jump in capacity to 33,000 TEUs, putting it in 31st position. Finally, the Indonesian feeder line, Samudera, a Singapore-registered company, came in at 40th position with 28 vessels amounting to 21,346 TEUs. It is clear from this that mergers and acquisitions continue apace, with a relatively small number of liner shipping companies operating as mega-carriers which are further strengthened by joining a handful of global shipping alliances. It appears that there are still niches available for the few enterprising liner companies holding out as regional operators.

Liberalization of maritime transport

The WTO has been pushing for greater liberalization of maritime transport services, albeit without success (Chia et al. 1999). The primary concern for a more liberal maritime transport regime is to create an altogether more efficient maritime transport system as part of the trend towards a freer economic structure as a whole. For the transport sector, the aim is to integrate shipping services to meet just-in-time (JIT) and door-to-door delivery requirements of shippers.

All countries must necessarily face the challenge of having continually to adjust their transport systems to cope with the rapidly increasing volume of cargo throughput. It is also essential that the transport system is capable of carrying goods reliably, safely and without damage or loss, providing JIT door-to-door delivery of goods, and point-to-point information to all interested parties. Economies that are unable to provide the services needed to facilitate speedier loading and discharge of cargo risk curtailment of trade. Liberalization has been identified as an effective way of bringing about the required improvements in the transport sector in order to support trade.

A related development is the promotion of inter-modalism, or multi-modalism involving the integration of all modes of transportation, and utilizing information technology (IT) and through close cooperation among all sub-sectors of the transport industry. The insistence of JIT and door-to-door services by shippers have also brought about a fundamental change in the pattern of shipping and, in part, resulted in the emergence of hub ports involving mega-carriers, similar to the developments which have occurred in the air transport sector. Shippers demand the required quantity of goods to arrive at their factories as near as possible to the time they are required for use, in order to avoid carrying high inventory costs and storing supplies expensively. Within the region, differences among nations in improving the capacity and reliability of inland transport systems have widened the gap between the few large and efficient sea ports and the smaller regional ones. Heavy expenses incurred in improving infrastructure have driven port operators to try to gain traffic from rival ports by widening the catchment for cargo and shipping services. This has inevitably heightened competition among ports.

Port competition has forced down port charges. In the case of freight rates, they are declining as a proportion of the value of goods transported. They represented 6.64 per cent of value in 1980, and 5.27 per cent in 1997. These costs are however higher for developing countries (8.3 per cent in 1997) than for developed countries (4.2 per cent). This gap can be explained by, among other factors, the higher value and larger volume of cargo employing bigger and more efficient ships (carrying up to 6,600 TEUs) in advanced countries compared to developing ones. There is also stronger competition from shipping lines serving developed markets. In addition, the average container load of a ship has more than doubled in the past two decades. Recent productivity indicators show a certain decline due to over-capacity. For many years there have been concerns expressed over the severe excess capacity of container ships although there is again considerable variation among the various trade routes.

In terms of the structure of the traffic, tanker traffic (the transport of both crude oil and refined products) accounts for 44.7 per cent in volume, dry bulk traffic (essentially the transport of iron ore, grain, coal, bauxite and phosphates) for 23 per cent, and liner traffic (the relatively high-value traffic mainly carried by container ships, roll-on–roll-off vessels and the remaining classic twin-decker cargo ships) for 32.6 per cent. In terms of the value of goods transported, the figures are higher for the liner trade due to the higher unit value of the goods transported. The proportion of the liner trade which is containerized is growing quickly by nearly 10 per cent per annum in the 1990s, and from 1998 to 2000 being 7 to 8 per cent, representing 55 per cent of liner trade. More than half of this traffic is now handled in the ports of developing countries.

Impact of the Asian financial crisis

The Asian financial crisis that began in mid 1997, starting in Thailand and quickly engulfing almost the entire Asian region, caused the economies of the region to contract drastically and the regional currencies to plunge in value. The collapse of many of the banking systems in the region and failure of large and small enterprises incapacitated normal trade and shipping. It resulted in a severe contraction of imports and expansion of exports. This adversely affected container trade by creating a huge imbalance of containers, requiring the repositioning of large numbers of non-revenue generating empty containers. This caused a large differential in freight rates in favour of inbound containers against outgoing containers and necessitated the imposition of repositioning surcharges. Surprisingly, container throughputs actually increased, (though at a reduced rate) during the period of recession, with the exception of inter-Asia container movements which declined by 5.8 per cent in 1998 (Table 1.7). West and eastbound container trade widened rapidly from 1997, with eastbound export trade growing by 53 per cent from 496 million TEUs to 7.61 million TEUs, while westbound import trade declined by 7 per cent from 4.33 million TEUs to 4.02 million TEUs from 1996 to 2000.

It has been estimated that, worldwide, 30 million TEUs of empty containers were handled at ports in 1996, and this number increased to 41 million TEUs in 1999. The same report mentioned that Hong Kong handled 3.4 million TEUs of empty containers, or 21 per cent of the total of 16.2 million TEU throughput, in 1999. In 1996, the number of empties was 2.4 million TEUs or 17.5 per cent of the total. In the case of Port Klang, the number of empties rose from 192,801 TEUs in 1996 to 424,590 TEUs in 1999, accounting for 13.7 and 17.7 per cent respectively of total throughput in the same years (IAPH Secretariat 2000).

TABLE 1.7
Container Trade on Major Asian Routes[a]

Route	Direction	1996	1997	1998	1999	2000[b]
Transpacific	Eastbound	4,959	5,723	6,845	7,610	8,237
	Westbound	4,333	4,463	3,839	4,016	4,368
	Total	9,292	10,187	10,684	11,626	12,605
	% change	8.8	9.6	4.9	8.8	8.4
Asia–Europe	Westbound	21,093	21,093	21,093	21,093	21,093
		2,565	3,798	3,342	3,533	3,860
	Eastbound	2,008	2,187	2,206	2,544	2,713
	Total	4,573	4,984	5,368	6,077	6,573
	% change	9.5	9.0	7.7	13.2	8.2
Inter-Asia	Total	7,228	7,796	7,343	8,150	8,590
	% change	3.3	7.9	–5.8	11.0	5.4
Total		**21,093**	**22,967**	**23,395**	**25,853**	**27,768**
Percent change		7.0	8.9	1.9	10.5	7.4

[a] Refers to loaded containers only.
[b] Estimates.
Source: Estimates by Korea Maritime Institute, quoted by IAPH Secretariat (2000).

This volume aims to provide the reader with an overview of shipping development in Southeast Asia framed within the context of world shipping development trends. Throughout the volume attention is focussed on containerized cargo and container ports in the region. Chapter 2 discusses port development policies in Southeast Asia, beginning with a review of the rapid changes occurring in the port environment due to technological advancements on the one hand and management of port operations on the other. Factors such as globalization and deregulation arising from greater liberalization of port services are explored. This leads to a discussion of strategies adopted by shipping lines, the operation of global ports and the implications for port functions and inter-port competition. The second section of Chapter 2 deals with port development policies and strategies adopted by ports in Southeast Asia, specifically the ports of Singapore, Klang in Peninsular Malaysia, Laem Chabang in Thailand, and Manila in the Philippines. The Port of Tanjung

Pelepas in the southern Malaysian state of Johor offers a special case study of port development strategy and competition posed against the hub port of Singapore. The chapter ends with a forward look at the status of various ports within the region.

The next three chapters are analytical in nature. Chapters 3 and 4 are analytical in their approach. In effect, Chapter 2 examines the operations of hub ports, specifically that of Singapore, as well as aspiring hub ports such as Port Klang and the Port of Manila. Past trends in world container volumes are first presented, followed by a forecast of future world container volumes in Chapter 4. This exercise takes into account world economic growth, trade liberalization, saturation of container markets and the increase in the unit value of containers. Country and regional forecasts of container cargo growth trends and patterns of transhipment follow this. From the analysis, a discussion of the status and role of regional growth hubs is presented.

Chapter 5 offers quite a different set of analytical tools, using mathematical models with inputs of known container ship specifications (sailing frequency, lead time and ocean freight) in regional and extra-regional ports to simulate different scenarios of the pattern of flows of containerized cargo affecting the countries in and surrounding Southeast Asia. This is achieved by changing the main parameters and then simulating for efficient container cargo flows. This provides the user with opportunities to examine the possible changes in various hub ports and the circumstances that influence these patterns and implications for existing, potentially major, and hub ports within the region. As a corollary, the strengths of hub ports within the Asian region are examined analytically using a simple flow model. An essential element of this is the operation of transhipment cargo, which may be regarded as the other side of the coin examined in Chapter 2.

The concluding chapter provides a summary of the overall intention and achievements of this book. In sum, the results of the analysis will have important implications for governments concerned with port development, providing insights into how they and port managers can develop strategies that will enhance the position of any particular port.

This volume thus lays out the essentials of the shipping and the status of ports of the countries in Southeast Asia, as well as of the major shipping countries in the surrounding region. It is also intended to provide a quick appreciation of the current shipping and port environment, as well as recent developments in the industry. The approach adopted is a comparative one which aims to bring out the competitive elements focussed on the operation of ports. The book should therefore be useful for policy-makers wishing to gain an appreciation of the dynamics and experience of existing hub ports, an insight into how their national ports can be strengthened and transformed into new hub ports and ideas of what is required to augment the flow of cargo through their ports.

Notes

1. *American Shipper*, July 2000, p. 92, quoted in ESCAP Secretariat (2000, p.17).
2. The Port of Kobe was, before the earthquake, the largest container port in Japan and was handling 2.7 million TEUs. Various berths were leased to more than 50 major international shipping lines. <www.eqe.com/publications/kobe/kobe.htm>
3. The Port of Singapore Authority (PSA) merged the regulatory departments, the Marine Department and the National Maritime Board, to form the Maritime and Port Authority (MPA) in 1996.

References

APEC (Asia-Pacific Economic Cooperation). *APEC Economic Outlook*. Report by the Economic Committee, Singapore: APEC Secretariat, 1995 and 1996.

APEC. *APEC EDI Pilot Project on Electronic Commerce*. Singapore: APEC Secretariat, 1995.

APEC. *Selected APEC Documents, 1989–1994*. Singapore: APEC Secretariat, 1996.

Brooks, Mary R. "Fleet development and the control of shipping in Southeast Asia", Occasional Paper no. 77. Singapore: Institute of Southeast Asian Studies, 1985.

Chia L.S. and Teresa Lim. "Shipping development in ASEAN: problems and prospects'. In *Southeast Asian Seas: Frontiers for Development*, edited by Chia Lin Sien and C. MacAndrews, pp. 179–204. Singapore: McGraw-Hill International, 1981.

Chia L.S., Lloyd C. Onyirimba and George S. Akpan. "Liberalization of maritime transport services: directions and options for Asia". Paper presented at conference, East Asia and Options for WTO 2000 Negotiations. PECC-TPF meeting in cooperation with the World Bank, 19–20 July 1999, Manila.

Containerisation International Yearbook. London: National Magazine Co., various years.

ESCAP. *Review of Developments in Transport, Communications and Tourism in the ESCAP Region*. New York: United Nations, 1995.

ESCAP (UN Economic and Social Commission for Asia and the Pacific). *Framework for the Development of National Shipping Policies*. United Nations, 1999.

Drewry Shipping Consultants. *Global Container Markets: Prospects and Profitability in a High Growth Era*. July 1996.

Drewry Shipping Consultants. *World Container Terminals: Global Growth and Private Profit*. April 1998.

Embassy of the United States of America. "Port of Singapore: the dominant regional hub". Economic/Political Section, mimeographed. Singapore, 1997.

Frank, B. and J.C. Bunel. "Contestability, Competition and Regulation — The Case of Liner Shipping". *International Journal of Industrial Organization* 9 (1991): 141–59.

Hamzah, A.B. "Malaysia: balancing regional concerns". In *Maritime Policy for Developing Nations*, edited by Greg Mills, pp. 258–63. The South African Institute of International Affairs (Johannesburg) and The Centre for Defence and International Security Studies. UK: Lancaster University, 1995.

International Association of Ports and Harbors (IAPH). "ESCAP Regional shipping and port development strategies under a changing maritime environment". In *Ports and Harbors*, December 2000, pp. 6–21.

Kang Jong-Soon and C. Findlay. "Prospects for Liberalization in Shipping Services". Paper presented at the International Conference on Ocean Economy and Sustainable Development in the APEC Region, organized by the Pacific Society of China; Xiamen Municipal Science and Technology Commission; Research School of Southeast Asian Studies, Xiamen University; and Southeast Asian Program in Ocean Law, Policy and Management (SEAPOL). 28–30 October 1998 Xiamen, China.

Lloyd's Registry of Shipping. *World Shipping Statistics*. London: Lloyd's Registry of Shipping, 1998.

Olsen, Barry K. "Container companies chart a global course". <www.ppl-mfi.com>, October 1999.

Seet-Cheng, Mary. "International Trends in Port Development". Paper presented at the International Conference on Ocean Economy and Sustainable Development in the APEC Region, organized by the Pacific Society of China; Xiamen Municipal Science and Technology Commission; Research School of Southeast Asian Studies, Xiamen University; and Southeast Asian Program in Ocean Law, Policy and Management (SEAPOL). 28–30 October 1998 Xiamen, China.

Shipping Times (Singapore), 19 January 2001. Donald Urquhart "Top 25 carriers make up half of global capacity".

Thomas B.J. "Structural changes in world economy and shipping". Seminar on Comparative Terminal Operations in South East Asia and Europe, organized by Port of Singapore Authority and Institute Portuaire Du Havre, 25–27 November 1996.

Trace, K. and L.S. Chia. "ASEAN and Australian shipping policies". In *Handmaiden of Trade: A Study on ASEAN–Australian Shipping*, edited by K. Trace, L.S. Chia, F.D. Gallagher and Shahril Abd. Hj. Karim, pp. 52–85. Singapore: Singapore University Press, 1988.

UNCTAD (United Nations Conference on Trade and Development). *Review of Maritime Transport 1997*. UNCTAD/RTM/97/1, 133, table 16, p. 29. Geneva: United Nations, 1997.

World Bank. *Lessons and Practices — Ports*. Operations Evaluation Department, report no. 9, June 1996.

World Trade Organisation. *Maritime Transport Services: Background Note by the Secretariat*. Council for Trade Services, 1998.

2

Port Development Policies in Southeast Asia: A Comparative Analysis

The external environment for ports is becoming more competitive. The forces of globalization, rapid advances in transport technology, and recent developments in the shipping industry have affected port operations and their bargaining position relative to that of the shipping lines. Some ports no longer enjoy a monopoly power over their hinterlands, as cargo originating from or destined for these places need not be shipped through them. On the other hand, shipping lines now have more choices of ports of call with the emergence of new ports and the expansion of port facilities to meet increasing freight traffic. This chapter will discuss the major trends that characterize the port environment, their implications for ports and the various development policies pursued by the major ports in the region in order to survive and thrive in this increasingly competitive environment.

Port environment

The port environment is increasingly becoming competitive due to the following factors: globalization, significant advances in transport technology and recent developments in the shipping industry.)

Globalization, brought about by the market liberalization policies pursued by most countries and by strategies adopted by many transnational corporations (which allocate the various aspects of the production process across countries based on their respective comparative advantages), has reinforced competition in the trading environment. This has put increasing pressure on ports, which constitute an important link in the trading chain, to improve their operational efficiency. It is no wonder then that port authorities have recently been turning their attention to improving their efficiency levels.

One _advance in transport technology_ which perhaps has most impacted the economics of sea transport has been the introduction of containerization. This has opened new routes linking various transport modes so as to offer more rapid and cost-efficient services. Thus, the traditional significance of the hinterland has been lost due to substantial improvements in efficiency in land transport and cargo handling. Containerization has facilitated the physical movement of freight across many transport modes, and thus ports can no longer ensure that cargo generated domestically will be handled at their terminals. Nor can a port expect to attract shipping lines just because it serves as a natural gateway to its hinterland. Shipping lines are now major agents of change in oceanic transportation, possessing a more varied choice of ports of call than ever before.

Developments in shipping industry.   Charges in operational strategies of shipping lines, including mergers and alliances and other forms of cooperation, such as vessel-sharing agreements, slot charter arrangements and consortia (alliances that are not on a global scale), due to highly competitive shipping markets have also contributed to greater inter-port competition. The question that begs an answer can be phrased as follows: is there a need for such alliances?

Containerization is capital-intensive and requires very high capital investment. About 80 per cent of the total costs involved in running container ships are fixed[1] (excluding marketing, administrative and other overhead costs). This large proportion of fixed costs in present vessels has resulted in very few shipping lines being able to afford to lay up a ship, since their costs continue to be incurred even when they are not in use. In contrast, the majority of the capital costs of conventional cargo ships are variable, and the lay-up of these ships is therefore less costly.

High capital costs are needed for establishing land-based operations to service container ships, such as door-to-door services and related operations. The capital-intensive containers require as many as six multi-million dollar cranes for their loading and unloading. Even before these capital costs are incurred, the initial huge sum of about US$60 million has to be paid just for the purchase of a container ship. When other costs are added in, the investment required becomes an exorbitant figure which can only be afforded through mergers.

Integration through competitive alliances enables several carriers to fill the mega-container ships of 8000-TEU capacity, whereas one carrier is unable to fill the ship by itself. A fully laden container ship is more cost-effective than a semi-filled one, since both incur the same amount of fixed costs, but a semi-filled ship suffers wastage of space and the resulting loss of revenue as well.

With alliances, economies of scale can be realized, resulting in lower operating costs and higher quality of services. In addition, a smooth flow of container services requires well-developed infrastructure, such as terminal infrastructure, and for one shipping line to provide these is infeasible. Through the pooling of resources in alliances, however, this can become a reality. Further, using big ships in alliances incurs lower costs through a reduction in the number of port calls, by concentrating as much cargo at each of the remaining ports as possible. This is something which one single shipping line is unable to achieve due to financing difficulties.

Lastly, the need to form alliances is also due to an increase in shipping line competition. The huge growth in world trade has attracted the influx of new players into the shipping industry. As shown in Chapter 1, traditional carriers like Sealand, APL, P&O,

Maersk, CGM, K-line, MOL, and OOCL are joined by carriers mainly from the East and Southeast Asia, such as Yangming, COSCO, MSC, Evergreen and Hanjin. As a result, shipping lines are pushed into restructuring to streamline their operations and lower overhead costs (through the various changes mentioned below) in order to keep pace with technology and their rivals.

The advent of strategic alliances of major container lines is partly a consequence of increasing ship size. The new generation of container ships is around 6,000 TEUs and ships of this size can be difficult to fill. Consequently, lines have pooled their operations to ensure that sufficient volumes of cargo are available. These alliances are effectively an extension of the consortia formed after the introduction of containerization. The original container consortia were created because general cargo shipping lines on individual routes had to band together to pay the very high costs associated with trade containerization. Later, lines experienced pressure to form closer alliances on major individual routes, to meet shipper requirements and give themselves greater flexibility. There are now few lines which do not at least slot charter to extend their service ranges. The major transatlantic, transpacific and Europe–Asia trades are now covered by the worldwide alliances that include ten of the top twenty carriers, which have already extended existing sectoral alliances. Other groups like Tricon (DSR-Senator, Cho Yang), Hanjin and UASC Cosco, K Line and Yang Ming have reciprocal slot arrangements.

The development of these alliances implies that more, not fewer, ports can be called at within the overall service. The massive pools of vessels in the alliances allow carriers to provide almost daily services between hub ports. They are, therefore, able to divide schedules into a number of "strings" which call at different port ranges. The crucial point is that the threshold volume of containers necessary to justify the first call with one of the strings is reached much earlier if an alliance, rather than an individual line, is picking up the cargo.

However, the trend among shipping lines to use very large ships, as part of their strategy to achieve economies of scale and reduce costs in an increasingly competitive shipping market, has resulted in fewer port calls. For example, the Mediterranean

Shipping Company (MSC) uses the Port of Felixstowe (UK) as its European export hub and the Port of Antwerp (Belgium) as its hub for European imports. It avoids additional ports of call through the employment of integrated land and ocean transport services (Fairplay 1997). The New World Alliance services its Asia–Europe route by calling at the Port of Singapore for its Southeast Asian market and the Port of Rotterdam for its European market. Table 2.1 illustrates the changes in ship size over the years.

This tendency of shipping lines to call at fewer ports has resulted in further concentration of port traffic in fewer and larger ports. These larger ships need certain port infrastructure and facilities, such as deeper draught and channels, better developed dock–rail connections and more extensive storage facilities. Smaller ports which have not yet invested in appropriate facilities

TABLE 2.1
Changes in Ship Size

	Dead weight tonnage (dwt)	TEUs
Tankers		
1945	16,500	
1950s	28,000	
1960s	70,000	
1970s	150,000–200,000 (VLCC)	
1980s	200,000–500,000 (ULCC)	
Bulk Carriers		
1950s	40,000	
1960s	80,000	
1970s	150,000–270,000	
1980s	270,000–350,000	
Containers		
First generation	15,000	750
Second generation	30,000	1,500–2,500
Third generation	50,000	3,000
Fourth generation	60,000	4,500–5,000
Panamax	65,000	

Source: Taken from various sources.

are forced to undertake heavy investments, or they lose their competitive advantage. But even for larger ports, where economies of scale can occur, investment in appropriate facilities is still a major issue, given the tight financial resources facing many countries, particularly in Southeast Asia. Apart from the port infrastructure requirements, this trend has also exerted greater pressure on smaller ports to attract more cargo and ship calls.

A growing proportion of containerized trade is being handled on a door-to-door basis, from the point of production to the point of consumption (Haynes et al. 1997). Most of this business is controlled by shipping lines that have turned into organizations engaged in logistics operations on a global scale. Ports are, therefore, becoming increasingly marginal in the routing of container flows.

The trend towards inter-modalism, which requires a complete logistical and distribution package to meet JIT functions (such as the need to offer warehousing and storage space, processing facilities and efficient inter-modal transfer and sophisticated information services), has also posed a major challenge to a port's traditional role of merely facilitating the movement of cargo from ship to shore.

Inter-modalism refers to the movement of containerized cargo from shipper to customer by at least two different modes of transport under a single freight rate. The objective is to bridge the gap between the origin of supply and the final destination of demand in the shortest time and most cost-effective way. The various forms of inter-modalism (Branch 1996) include:

1.   Containerization (FCL/LCL/road/sea/rail)
2.   Land bridge via trailer/truck (road/sea/road)
3.   Land bridge via pallet/IATA container (road/sea/air/road)
4.   Trailer/truck (road/sea/road)
5.   Swapbody (road/rail/sea/road).

Inter-modalism (also referred to as multi-modalism) arises out of the evolution of containerization. It has been mentioned that the container provides the technical basis for the new inter-modalism (Hayuth 1987). With cargo packed into containers, this increases the ease of transporting cargo from one destination to another using different transport modes. Unlike the conventional transport system in which each mode of transport acts independently, inter-modality intensifies and brings closer together different modes of transport. However, caution must be exercised in the stowing of the containerized cargo as, improperly stowed, it can damage the cargo. This will defeat the purpose of transporting cargo in containers.

Besides containers, there are other types of inter-modal transport modes, such as "bridge" services — namely, the landbridge, minibridge and microbridge. These bridges use transatlantic and transpacific water transport combined with a rail piggyback to move goods across the North American continent (Mahoney 1985), and they are in use all around the world.

Carriers decide the routing to be used in connection with minibridge and microbridge rates and tend to divert all the traffic through a port that offers the best rates. Thus, business will be diverted away from ports whose rates are uncompetitive.

Unlike the inter-modal bridge services, which constitute a combination of sea and land transport modes, another common form of inter-modal transport, which consists solely of land transport modes, and is known as the "ocean–rail" transport. Containers are stacked on rail cars or the so-called "double-stack" trains. This mode of transport concentrates shipping activities only at selected ports, and tends to intensify inter-port competition, as ports to compete in order to be one of the few selected.

Inter-modalism changes the role of the port, from servicing break-bulk cargo to becoming a link in an entire transport chain. Cargo is unloaded at the ports and transferred to various points using different transport modes. Ports therefore form the link with other transport modes such as ocean, rail, roads and even air transport.

The evolution of large multi-modal transport companies as a result of inter-modality brings turbulent waves into the transportation industry, linking various transport modes together — a big contrast to the past. These large multi-modal transport companies provide shippers with a controlled and coordinated international movement of containerized cargo through a system that links together all three surface transportation modes, ocean, rail and truck, and possibly air transportation as well (Hoyle and Knowles 1992). With this coordination and efficient channelling of cargo through various modes, duplication of administrative expenses and facilities is eliminated, resulting in larger cost savings.

Inter-modalism has also been described as an operation in which computers play an influential role, electronic data interchange through (EDI). EDI is defined as the application-to-application exchange of computer-held information in a structural format via a telecommunications network (Branch 1996). In simpler terms, it is a paperless trading across all borders; no manual printing of documents is needed, and all information is transmitted via telecommunications. EDI facilitates inter-modalism, and most shipping lines use it, — some have even come up with several improvements.

In summary, the above trends have not only reduced the bargaining power of ports *vis-à-vis* the shipping lines, but have also resulted in the following: greater inter-port competition as shipping alliances rationalize and choose to call at fewer ports where economies of scale can be achieved; increased concentration in port systems as hub ports continue to attract more cargo and regional feeder ports get less and less traffic volume; and reordering of the position of ports and change in port hierarchical structure as a result of increased transhipment and significant increase in the demand for expensive and modern infrastructure and superstructures.

Regional port development policies and strategies

Singapore

The Port of Singapore has established itself as the region's premier container hub port. The port holds the honour of being the world's busiest container port, achieving a throughput of 15.14 million TEUs in 1998, surpassing the port of Hong Kong. In 2000, the port's container throughput grew by 6.5 per cent, reaching a record 17.04 million TEUs (*The Straits Times* 2001). The PSA Corporation is the world's single largest container terminal owner–operator. It handles about one tenth of the world's container throughput (*Asia Times* 2000). Most of this traffic is transhipment — that is, either originating from or destined for countries outside of Singapore. This is not surprising given the limited size of the domestic market. It has been reported that about 50 per cent of Malaysian sea cargo goes via the Port of Singapore (*Shipping Times*, 16 October 1997). In dollar terms, some RM164 billion worth of goods are dispatched by Malaysian exporters a year through the port of Singapore (The New Straits Times 1998). In 1990, approximately 70 per cent of its 4 million TEUs was accounted for by containers transhipped from neighbouring ports (Airriess 1993). Large ships do not have to call at every port within the region, but only at the port of Singapore to unload into or load cargo from feeder ships. This enables the shipping lines not only to cut their costs but also to provide a high frequency of service, maximize the utilization of slots of the mother vessels and to have a broad choice of feeders. From the viewpoint of shippers, this system allows them a wider choice of shipping lines and times at more competitive rates.

To give some indication of the extent to which the port of Singapore relies on transhipment, Table 2.2 shows the proportion of transhipment to total throughput in selected major ports based on 1996 data. As can be gleaned from Table 2.2, its proportion of transhipment came fourth highest after the ports of Malta, Algeciras, and Damietta, but certainly is the highest among the major transhipment hubs such as the ports of Hong Kong, Rotterdam, Kaohsiung and Felixstowe.

Under the PSA, Singapore has seen spectacular growth. From a conventional port, it has remained the world's busiest port in terms of shipping tonnage, attracting over 1,000,000 vessel calls registering over 700 million gross tonnes a year. As Table 2.2 shows, it holds the honour of being one of the world's largest transhipment hubs, with links to over 400 shipping lines and over 600 ports worldwide.

Originally established as a statutory board under the Ministry of Communications in 1964, the PSA has been corporatized since October 1997. Corporatization is aimed at freeing the PSA from

TABLE 2.2

Proportion of Transhipments to Total throughput in Major Ports, 1996

Ports	Transhipments as percentage of total throughput
1. Malta	92
2. Algeciras	90
3. Damietta	90
4. Singapore	78
5. Kingston	75
6. Colombo	72
7. Gioia Tauro	65
8. Dubai	48
9. Kaohsiung	43
10. Rotterdam	40
11. Antwerp	35
12. Hamburg	35
13. Busan	30
14. Felixstowe	28
15. Bremerhaven	25
16. Hong Kong	20
17. Kobe	15

Source: Various published data on ports.

the encumbrances of a government body to allow it to be more commercially focused and customer oriented. Thus, it is now in a better position to provide customized services for individual clients. Although the PSA Corporation is currently handling all operations of the port, there are plans to open the port to competition for contracts and bids for further development in future.

To maintain its position as the region's hub port, the port of Singapore has adopted a two-pronged strategy: capitalizing on its area of comparative strengths, and forging more cooperative alliances with other ports. The first stage of this strategy has been to improve the port's infrastructure, level of efficiency and quality of services. Under its massive infrastructure programme, the PSA tries to ensure that its port facilities are adequate to handle future increases in cargo traffic and ship visits by investing in port expansion and upgrading. The almost completed development of the Pasir Panjang terminal, which opened in 1998 (after completing the first phase of the project), has given an extra handling capacity of 18 million TEUs. Once this terminal becomes fully operational, the port's total container handling capacity is expected to be roughly 36 million TEUs per annum. In addition, the port's terminals are supported by a number of distribution parks, providing over half a million square metres of warehousing in total. (A distribution park is a large covered warehouse which provides automated storage facilities.) Here, customers can process their documents, pack and unpack, mark, label and assemble their goods for distribution to other distribution centres.

To improve efficiency and quality of service, the Port of Singapore has capitalized on its comparative strength in the areas of IT and human resources. The port uses the latest IT in every aspect of administration, planning and operations services. Its EDI system is used to plan berth allocation, ship towage and yard management. For example, PORTNET provides one-stop convenience for all transactions and linking all port users with related shipping agencies. All containers relayed through the Port of Singapore are systematically sorted out for distribution to the second carriers. Advanced cargo-handling equipment, such as fourth generation quay cranes, double-trolley cranes and double-stack trailers are used. The current management is further upgrading its cargo-handling technology by almost entirely automating its terminal operations. In the new Pasir Panjang terminal containers are handled and transported by computer-controlled machines. The port management is currently using automatic guided vehicles capable of navigating autonomously and stacking containers by remote-controlled bridge cranes. Apart from its present containers and vessels automated tracking system, the management has recently implemented a system whereby shipping and cargo information can be accessed through the Internet.

The Port of Singapore has consistantly tried to maintain close relations with its clients, especially the shipping lines. By conducting regular meetings with its clients, the PSA is kept up-to-date on their needs and complaints so as to provide them with more customized services. A Key Customer Manager (KCM) is in charge of looking after individual customer needs and complaints and to work out solutions to fulfil their requirements. A series of cost reduction measures has been implemented as a result from these regular meetings. For example, the 20 per cent concession in port dues for container ships (except long-standing ships) was extended into 1998 and 1999 (*Shipping Times*, 5 August 1997).

The PSA has also embarked on the strategy of signing contracts with shipping lines to ensure their continued patronage in the near future. For example, the Virtual Terminal (VT) contract, which the PSA signed with the Global Alliance[2] on 12 August 1996, guarantees the PSA this alliance's shipping business for ten years. The VT contract is the world's first contract of this type, and will cater to these shipping lines' different logistical requirements. It also promises reliability of service, greater customization, price stability and cost effectiveness (PSA Press Releases, 12 August 1996).

The Port of Singapore has also been promoting itself as a total logistics centre where door-to-door services are available with state-of-the-art logistical facilities. It shows how it can add value to the activities of the shipping lines by promoting its bunkering industry, ship registry and other marine-related activities including marine finance, insurance, brokerage and other services that make the port a one-stop centre. As a result, the Singapore Registry of Ships has grown rapidly in recent years and today ranks as the seventh largest in the world. To attract ship-owners to set up base in Singapore, the Trade and Development Board has implemented since 1991 an attractive incentive scheme, the Approved Shipping Enterprise Scheme (AIS). Companies under this scheme enjoy a tax exemption of up to ten years on income earned from qualifying shipping operations. To qualify for the scheme, 10 per cent of the company's fleet has to be registered with the Singapore flag. The scheme has proved a strong draw for some of the world's top shipping companies, with 36 AIS companies operating a total of more than 500 vessels using Singapore as a base.

Singapore has a thriving ship-financing community, with shipping banks such as ING, Christiana Bank and MeesPierson joining a local player, the Development Bank of Singapore. Progress has also been made in building up the local insurance industry. Two P&I Clubs, the Standard Club and the UK Club, now have regional offices in Singapore. Lloyds is continuing negotiations to set up an underwriting presence in the Republic.

Further, it endeavours to increase the profile of the Port of Singapore internationally by actively participating in the activities of the IMO to safeguard its strategic maritime interests and keep the sea safe and open to navigation. It also does so by establishing links with other like-minded countries, by inviting certain prominent individuals to the country as part of international advisory groups and also as distinguished visitors.

The second approach follows the policy of active engagement with other ports. Apart from marketing its consultancy services internationally, particularly in IT-based port operations and port terminal logistics management, the port of Singapore has forged cooperative ventures with other ports as far away as China, India and Africa, offering capital and expertise in developing and managing state-of-the-art ports. Through these overseas ventures it hopes to build up stronger port linkages with other countries via the hub-spoke networks. The Port of Singapore aims to achieve 20 per cent of its annual revenue derived from these overseas ventures, particularly from various strategic alliances and investments in the logistics business and port terminal development. It is currently involved in projects in China, India, Indonesia, Vietnam, South Korea, Hong Kong, Italy and Brunei. In this way it can maintain its position as a hub by having greater influence on the supply of transhipment cargo from other ports in the region. These partnerships have so far shown positive results; for example, the PSA's joint venture project with the Port of Dalian Authority in Northeast China saw an increase of 11 per cent in 1998. The PSA has handled 1.5 million TEUs overseas and aims to handle at least 10 million TEUs by year 2007 and to earn at least a third of its revenue from overseas projects (*PSA Annual Report 1998*).

Through these partnerships, the PSA can reap benefits. Firstly, by forming partnerships with ports (those which have the potential of becoming hub ports), the PSA is guaranteed of a source of revenue. The PSA's joint venture with the Middle East to construct the Aden Container Terminal in Yemen, which has the potential to become the region's most efficient and advanced container terminal hub, will guarantee the PSA of a viable source of revenue. Secondly, such alliances are a form of diversification. Rather than relying simply on its own port, the PSA now has the back-up of other ports. In the event that Port of Singapore were to lose its competitiveness, the PSA still has these overseas ports to fall back on. Thirdly, partnerships with other ports also enhance the PSA's partnerships with major shipping lines through cooperation in overseas port projects. This has helped the PSA to weather the recent Asian financial crisis. The crisis resulted in a considerable reduction in imports coming into Southeast Asian markets, leading to less containers arriving at a time when the demand for containers was high due to a surge in exports to the West. To salvage this situation, the PSA used its joint efforts with various shipping lines to bring in more cargo from China, Australia/New Zealand and South Asia, thus managing to secure a double-digit growth for the PSA (*ibid.*). The revenue gained from these port joint ventures in turn enabled the PSA to give out rebates and simplify port tariffs for clients.

By forming partnerships with overseas ports, the PSA has not only diversified its investment but has also improved its competitiveness by awarding rebates and employing other cost reduction measures from the revenue earned through overseas investments. Should the PSA's charges be higher than those of regional ports, the shippers are compensated in the form of rebates and other cost reduction measures.

Furthermore, the PSA is not only involved in overseas projects, but it is also diversifying into other businesses. The PSA is now partnering with the port of Dalian Authority to redevelop the eastern area of Dalian Port into a modern waterfront leisure and business hub (ibid.).

Tanjung Pelepas

Even though the PSA has undertaken various strategies to improve its competitiveness, and has come up with innovative ideas to give the port of Singapore an edge over the competition, other ports in the region are also doing the same.

As part of the Malaysian government's plan to recapture its cargo traffic, which being shipped through the Port of Singapore, and to rival Singapore as the region's hub port, a port was set up located about 45 minutes from the region's international shipping lanes. Since the beginning of its operations in 2000, it has already attracted four main shipping lines, Maersk-Sealand APL-NOL, K-line and Mitsui OSK Lines, to call at its port. The recent relocation of Maersk-Sealand, the world's biggest container shipping line, from Singapore to this port has provided a big boost to the port's transhipment status.

Apart from its good location, the port also enjoys a naturally deep water of 15 metres supported by a 12.6 km-long approach channel 250 metres in width, and a 600 metre turning basin which allows for a two-way passage of vessels and quick turnaround of vessel transit time. Like the Port of Singapore, it uses start-of-the-art IT and equipment, which gives every port user instant access to the port's purpose-designed integrated terminal and port management information system (ITPMIS). By synergizing all the port's operations and communication centres, the ITPMIS facilitates a free flow of updated information and provides near paperless transactions between the port personnel, shipping lines, marine services and freight forwarders. An automated gate system, berth allocation, ship planning and yard planning have also been fully computerized for smooth flow and reduced waiting time. An on-line container-status inquiry, history and tracking system can track cargo through the port from the moment it arrives.

The new port is reportedly moving aggressively to achieve its goal of securing a position as Southeast Asia's premier transhipment hub. As at the Port of Singapore, transhipments make up the bulk of business at Tanjung Pelepas, with transhipped containers accounting for 85 per cent of its total throughput in 2000. To achieve this goal, the management has focussed on securing main liners as well as feeder operators to call at the port by offering incentives: dedicated berths to certain customers, and the same level of service and efficiency as the PSA but at 30 per cent lower cost (*Shipping Times* 2000). Compared to Singapore, Malaysia can offer lower rates due to cheaper labour costs, the availability of land and government incentives. As a result, it has already gained some 2 million TEUs a year from Maersk and a growing number of feeder operators have expressed keen interest (*Shipping Times Online* 2000).

The Malaysian Ministry of Finance, in a bid to increase port throughput, has lifted a levy on container trucks ferrying goods from Singapore to Tanjung Pelepas, as well as on trucks transporting goods that arrive at Tanjung Pelepas bound for Singapore. Raising the levy on trucks ferrying containers to Singapore is currently under consideration. It is estimated that more than 2000 trucks move goods from Johor to Singapore daily, carrying almost 1 million TEUs a year to Singapore. Malaysia hopes to stop this leak (*Journal of Commerce* 2001).

The Malaysian government has also made it easier for cargo to be channelled from the Port of Pasir Gudang to the Port of Tanjung Pelepas by doing away with detailed customs procedures and other documentation, when cargo is transported from Pasir Gudang in eastern Johor to the Port of Tanjung Pelepas in the west for subsequent export (*Shipping Times* 2001).

Port Klang

Port Klang, the largest port in Malaysia, is located on the west coast of Peninsular Malaysia in the state of Selangor. It is only 40 km from the capital, Kuala Lumpur. This position supposedly makes it the first port of call for ships on the eastbound leg and the last port of call on the westbound leg of the Far East–Europe trade. It serves a hinterland covering major existing and planned growth areas in Selangor. Encompassing an area of 806 hectares and comprising the North Port, the West Port and the South Port, it offers comprehensive state-of-the-art facilities and services for handling cargo of all types. The three gateways encompass a total berth length, both existing and under planned development, of 16 km. They have sophisticated back-up facilities such as post-Panamax quay cranes, RTGs and straddle carriers that can handle up to 1.05 million TEUs.

All of the port's operational services have been privatized in line with the government's privatisation policy. The Klang Container Terminal (KCT) in the North Port is the first privatized container terminal in the country. Klang Multi Terminal, operating at the West Port, is 30 per cent owned by Hutchinson Whampoa's Hong Kong International Terminal (HIT).

The three container terminals have a total capacity of 3.6 million TEUs per annum and are expected to handle 4.4 million TEUs by the year 2010. The port handled around 3.2 million TEUs in 2000, and was ranked 14 in the list of top container ports in the world. Table 2.3 shows the spectacular growth of containers handled at this port over the five-year period from 1995 to 2000.

Transhipment has also been growing, accounting for 37 per cent of the port's total volume in 1999. This growth was fostered by the increased trade between Port Klang and regional ports including Penang, Jakarta, Yangon and Bangkok. Rail-bound cross-border container traffic from and to Bangkok is expected to be an important source of transhipment traffic at Port Klang via the cross-border container landbridge linking Port Klang and Bangkok. More shipping lines are beginning to consider the advantage of the cross-border land bridge service compared to an all-blue water feedering. Shipping lines that are already making use of this service include P&O Nedlloyd, Evergreen and Hanjin Shipping. Port Klang is also linked by ten daily block train services to various dry ports and sea ports in the country.

TABLE 2.3
Containers Handled at Port Klang, 1995–2000

Year	Loaded	Empty	Total
1995	986,862	146,949	1,133,811
1996	1,216,793	192,801	1,409,594
1997	1,452,884	231,624	1,684,508
1998	1,466,261	353,757	1,820,018
1999	1,960,353	590,066	2,550,419
2000	2,551,553	655,220	3,206,753

Source: Klang Port Authority web site.

The Malaysian government envisions Port Klang becoming the hub centre for national and regional traffic. To realize the objective of transforming this port into the country's load centre and alternative hub for the region, the following strategies have been adopted. First, to establish a strong cargo base the government, the port authority and the private terminal operators have pursued aggressive marketing and promotional programmes, dialogues, visits to clients and negotiations to ensure both indigenous and regional transhipment traffic are made available in the port. They have established distriparks and warehousing facilities in close proximity to the port, and inland clearance depots and dry ports at strategic locations around the country. Two distribution parks, Port Klang Distribution Park at the North Port and the West Port Distribution Park, offer purpose-built facilities for packing and repacking, sorting and grading, break-bulking, labelling and distribution activities. In addition, supply-driven approach has been adopted in the provision of port infrastructure to ensure port facilities are available in anticipation of increased demand and to ensure that the cargo owners are given facilities and services on arrival to minimize waiting time.

Second, to attract more main shipping-line operators (MLOs), they have offered incentives in the form of rebates, volume discounts and waiver of certain port charges (such as for pilotage and tugboats). The Port Klang Authority is offering a RM20 (S$9.12) rebate for each twenty-foot container and RM35 for each 40-foot container, as well as a 10 per cent discount on marine charges including pilotage and tugboat services. The need to increase shipping frequencies and ease of connection to other ports is important in order to attract more cargo owners to use the port. Port Klang currently provides direct trade links to more than 300 ports worldwide in about 120 countries, through the 60 MLOs who provide regular shipping frequencies on a daily and weekly basis. Third, the port has continuously improved its inland inter-modal connections through the maintenance of a network of highways and railways. Fourth, to ensure that efficient services are available at competitive prices, port charges have been maintained at their existing levels while the turnaround time of vessels and cargo dwelling times have been consistently improved. Fifth, port transactions are simplified and made more transparent through automation and computerization. The implementation of EDI has made port transactions, such as pre-clearance of customs, immigration and health, paperless and much quicker. To encourage transhipment activities and other value-added services, free commercial zones have been established. Both the North Port and the West Port are now gazetted as free commercial zones to allow activities such as direct transhipment, storage, consolidation and distribution, trading activities and value-added services. The cabotage policy has been amended to encourage shipping lines to consolidate cargo traffic in the port. Equity participation of foreign shipping operators has been increased to 70 per cent to enhance the port's appeal as a regional office for foreign shipping lines.

The Klang Port Authority (KPA), a statutory body created by an Act of Parliament on 1 July 1963 to take over all port operations from the Malaysian Railway Administration, has pursued a series of privatization programmes to achieve higher efficiency and productivity, to relieve the government of financial and administrative burdens, to reduce the size and presence of the public sector in the economy and to help meet the national economic policy targets.[3] The container terminal (KCT) was privatized in March 1986, while the remaining operational services at the initial gateways, the North Port and the South Port, were privatized in December 1992. The new gateway, the West Port, was privatized in September 1994. Privatization has enabled Klang to have access to foreign capital, management know-how and state-of-the-art technology. As a result, its performance has improved. The average container handling rate per ship hour increased from 35 TEUs before 1986 to 51 TEUs in 1998. Ship turnaround time improved from 12.5 hours to 11 hours during the same period (*Container Asia* 1998). Overall turnaround time also improved, from 101 hours before privatization to 79 hours after privatization (Kadir 1996).

The other contributing factor to the port's significant performance is that it is located in the most industrialized and populated economic region of Malaysia. All factories can be reached within eight hours, and the KPA is only 40 km away from Kuala Lumpur. In addition, within the port there is a whole range of marine services, including bunkering, ship chandlers and supplies, ship repairs and seamen's facilities.

Laem Chabang

Laem Chabang Port (LCP) was established in 1991 to combat port congestion in the Port of Bangkok due to the rapid increase in the volume of containerized cargo. Unlike the Bangkok port, which is purely under government control, LCP is managed and operated under the Public–Private Partnership. The switch to partial private control is due to the usual flaws of any enterprise under government control. This deep-sea commercial port is located at the eastern shore of the upper Gulf of Thailand, approximately 110 km south of Bangkok. LCP is a new modernized business port and has supposedly become the most efficient gateway port of Thailand.

Today, LCP operates 11 terminals to accommodate various types of vessels, including container ships, bulk carriers, pure car carriers and passenger liners. Among these, five are container terminals (B1 to B5); another three are the Coastal Terminal (A1), the Bulk Terminal (A4) and the General Cargo Terminal (A5); and the rest are under design and construction (A0, A2 and A3). More than 80 per cent of sea-borne cargo handled by LCP is containerized.

The Port of Thailand Authority (PAT) is trying to facilitate Laem Chabang Port becoming a hub port for services between Southeast Asia and North America. To achieve this, the PAT plans to carry out three phases of LCP development under its privatization programme. Phase 1 aims to maximize throughput per terminal handled by private operators. So far, the results obtained are positive. In 1998, imports, exports and transhipment cargo handled at LCP totalled 8,602 million tons, an increase of about 46 per cent from 1997. Of this 46 per cent improvement, 44 per cent was due to the increase in the volume of containerized cargo handled. Between 1996 and 1997, containerized cargo grew by 42.2 per cent from 728,630 TEUs to 1,036,063 TEUs despite the

Asian economic crisis, and in 1998 grew by 37.5 per cent to 1,424,702 TEUs. In addition, the frequency of ship calls also increased by about 52 per cent from 817 calls in 1997 to 2,378 calls in 1998 (Port of Thailand Authority web site).

To meet cargo demands until the year 2018, LCP has set out a master plan including phase 2 and phase 3 development. This will entail the expansion of its capacity and other facilities. Under phase 2, six container terminals and a passenger terminal with a total berth length of 4,100 m will be constructed by the year 2008.

The six additional container terminals under phase 2 development will be built in four stages. Stage 1 (C3 terminal), completed at the end of 1999, provides a 500-metre-long terminal with a capacity of 600,000 TEUs. This terminal is designed to accommodate at least one post-Panamax vessel and one feeder vessel simultaneously. Upon completion of phase 2, LCP's annual capacity will be 5 million TEUs.

In preparation for phase 2, the PAT takes into account the size of post-Panamax vessels as well as logistical services to respond rapidly to customer needs. On 5 March 1997, LCP recorded a success when its first post-Panamax vessel of 5,250 TEUs docked at its port (*ibid.*).

In addition, the PAT has also developed inter-modal transport. For example, there are plans for an efficient inter-modal transport system, such as using a double track railway and a highway network, as this will give the port the ability to facilitate faster and more efficient cargo consolidation or deconsolidation, storage and regional redistribution of cargo. This strategy also offers a comprehensive attraction to the direct call of shipping lines. Plans to improve port service roads, including the construction of flyover bridges at the crossing points between highways or railways, conforming to the main road network capacity and the development programme, are also in the pipeline.

Although LCP has undertaken a series of upgrading programmes in its port facilities, simplifying customs procedures and other measures, there is still some room for improvement, especially in the area of inland traffic. Road traffic congestion may delay the transportation of containerized cargo, and can act as a deterrent to potential clients from using LCP. Even though LCP is not affected by this traffic congestion (because it is located near the highways which lead to northern part of Thailand and bypasses Bangkok), port-related services such as banking and insurance, which are core commercial businesses, are mostly located in Bangkok. Thus, solving this traffic congestion problem should be made one of the port's immediate priorities.

Manila

Due to its unique geographical configuration comprising more than 7000 islands, the Philippines is immensely dependent on water transport for its trade and commerce. Ports handle almost 98 per cent of the materials and products imported and exported by the Philippines. Hence, the Philippine ports play a vital role, acting as an essential interface between land and sea transport and therefore making them catalysts for economic growth. Current development efforts are centred on 42 ports nationwide, which have been identified by the Philippine Ports Authority (PPA) in its master plan as crucial to economic development. These ports are slated for major development in infrastructure and landslide equipment to enhance their competitive global advantage. To achieve this aim, the government has undertaken the development of existing national ports as well as the construction of new ports, in line with the drive to become globally competitive in the country's transportation sector. Recognizing the present dilapidated condition of the country's ports, the government has tapped into the private sector to operate and maintain port facilities, with the PPA acting as a regulatory agency.

Although new laws have been implemented new vessels acquired, the country's present port facilities are still insufficient to cope with the escalating volume of passenger and container traffic. Thus there is a need to develop and improve port facilities, maritime safety and pollution control facilities, as well as to enhance the management capabilities of the PPA. In the next three years, the government will upgrade and develop maritime safety and pollution control facilities and capabilities through the Global Maritime and Distress and Safety System project. A vessel tracking system is also currently being implemented. The government has likewise identified priority infrastructure projects relating to the rehabilitation and improvement of the port and its facilities. Construction of new ports will be limited to private ports catering to specialized cargo commodities.

Over the next twenty-five years, the PPA will work towards the development of selected major ports to serve as service centres or hub ports. Offering a comprehensive transport package to include storage, distribution and information support, special amenities such as passenger terminals with restaurants, communication facilities and recreational areas will be constructed. Computer-based systems and procedures will become standard service in the bigger ports. Smaller ports will not lose their relevance but will be developed as multi-purpose terminals capable of handling both break-bulk and boxed cargo. These ports will form the link between the service centres or hubs and the hinterland. The coming age of multi-modalism will push ports to provide the major interface between land and sea. Thus, future investments of the PPA will be aimed at situating port facilities in locations where they complement and integrate smoothly with other transport modes. In addition, the PPA will develop specialized terminal for containers, bulk and passengers.

In the medium term (fifteen-year) master plan, the PPA expects growth to be still centred around Metro Manila, although there will be gradual emergence of new growth centres in the southern corridor in view of the industrial developments in the Cavite-Laguna-Batangas-Rizal-Quezon (CALABARZON) area and in Cebu.

In the light of an anticipated growth in traffic and increasingly competitive environment, the PPA plans to develop the port of Manila into a regional hub port. Under this plan, dredging of the entrance channel and the waters along the berths is scheduled to commence this year. The port of Manila is the country's largest port, accounting for a very substantial portion of the country's domestic and international trade. Apart from serving Metro Manila, the country's industrial heartland, it is also the national load centre. It consists of three terminals: the North Harbour for domestic bulk, break-bulk and containerized cargo; the South

Harbour for international bulk, break-bulk and containerized cargo, and the Manila International Container Terminal for international containerized cargo. However, the port has no capacity to accommodate very large vessels, which require a depth of at least 14 metres, since the depth of its entrance channel is only 10.5 metres while the alongside berth depth is only around 12 metres deep. Thus, cargo originating from or bound for major international markets are being transhipped via the ports of Singapore, Hong Kong and Kaohsiung.

Under the five-year plan of Subic Bay, the Subic Bay management has also envisioned building another container port in Subic Bay to serve as a regional hub. To be managed by a private operator, this port will capitalize on its locational advantage (close to Northeast Asia), excellent infrastructure and naturally deep harbour.

Tanjung Priok

The increase in containerization led Tanjung Priok in Indonesia to face port congestion in 1993 and 1994, incurring heavy losses for the shippers. To solve this problem, Koja Container Terminal (TPK Koja) was constructed for the expansion of port facilities and infrastructure, under the Public–Private Partnership scheme.

To compete with other ports, Tanjung Priok has undertaken several port developments. For example, TPK Koja is now equipped with post-Panamax cranes to service the mega-container ships. In fact, TPK Koja is now capable of handling container vessels with capacity of 3,500–5,000 TEUs. To improve its port services, state-of-the-art technology has also been implemented. Tanjung Priok has a Vessel Traffic Information System for monitoring the traffic flow and providing navigational safety. Online vessel service and cargo handling systems have also been implemented to improve efficiency levels in berthing services. There is also a one-stop service centre catering for client services.

In terms of inter-modal transportation, shippers can either use the highway or the railway for transporting containerized cargo. Also, Tanjung Priok is linked to various areas such as Jakarta for port-related services for port users' convenience.

In sum, major ports in the region have adopted port development policies and strategies that are generally aimed at expanding and upgrading their port infrastructure. For most ports, access to state-of-the-art technology and management has been realised through privatization. Except for in Singapore, in the development of the ports' respective infrastructures little attention has been given to the social aspects of infrastructure and to the need for cooperative endeavours among ports in the region.

The future direction of regional port development

With increased inter-port competition and the trend towards inter-modalism, ports will focus on logistics rather than simply on the provision of port infrastructure. Cargo that requires multiple transport modes in order to be transported from its point of origin to its destination in the shortest possible time and at the minimum cost has to go through several stages of repacking, recording, storage and other procedures. The use of logistics will expedite this process and optimise the performance of this cargo transfer between transport modes. Another method of optimizing cargo transfer is the JIT method, which is adopted to avoid the untimely arrival of cargo, incurring logistics costs. This method operates on tight delivery schedules to ensure that cargo arrives on time.

Realizing the importance of EDI programmes, individual companies have been coming up with very advanced computerized communication systems to attract more shippers. Maersk Line has a propriety system known as MAGIC, which enables shippers to track the movement of their cargo from the time Maersk Line accepts the cargo until this cargo reaches its destination. To keep up with competition, Hanjin Shipping has a computerized online real-time system, which links up all the networks of the company across the world, providing a global logistics service to all clients.

With shipping lines introducing more and more advanced EDI programmes, ports will have to provide similar services to prevent these lines from shifting their business elsewhere. In fact, ports have been competing with one another in the introduction of even more advanced electronic systems, hoping to be the first in implementing a new system to gain first-mover advantage.

With more carriers offering logistical services and carrying larger volumes of varied cargo, the demand for specialized terminals has increased. The main objective of having specialized terminals is to provide a wide range of value-added services, such as door-to-door delivery, repacking and container repair.

In addition, there is also a need to further develop other related services, such as insurance companies, legal and banking services, so as to make the usage of port services more convenient for shippers. For example, several business parks have been created to provide trade and distribution centres to service foreign countries. In the port of Guadeloupe for example, in addition to the usual port services and port-related activities, other value-added services are offered to increase the port's attractiveness, such as exhibition facilities, conference equipment and even language consultants (UNCTAD 1990).

To combat increasing competition, ports need to upgrade their infrastructure as well as to develop increasingly advanced services to improve their productivity and efficiency, so as to lower port charges and increase their competitiveness. In addition, they will continually have to try to come up with new gimmicks in their attempts to attract shippers.

Notes

1. Fixed costs are costs which are incurred once a voyage commences irrespective of the volume of cargo handled. They include costs like depreciation and interest payments on loans undertaken for shipbuilding.
2. This Global Alliance is the combination of American President Lines, Mitsui OSK Lines, Nedlloyd Lines and Orient Overseas Container Lines.
3. The ports in Malaysia came under five main federal port authorities, namely the Penang Port Commission, Klang Port Authority, Kuantan Port Authority, Johor Port Authority and Bintulu Port Authority. Each authority was created under laws specifically enacted by the Malaysian Parliament for such purpose.

References

Airriess, Christopher. "Export-oriented Manufacturing and Container Transport". *Geography* 78, no. 1 (1993): 34.

Asia Times, September 2000. Tony Allison, "A New Era in Asian Shipping". From web site, *Asia Times online:* www.atimes.com/se-asia/B102Ae03.html.

Branch, Alan E. *Elements of Shipping*. 7th ed. United Kingdom: St Edmundsbury Press, 1996.

Fairplay (London), 6 February 1997, pp. 26–27. Fairplay Publications Ltd.

Haynes, K.E. et al. "Regional Port Dynamics In the Global Economy: The case of Kaohsiung, Taiwan". *Maritime Policy and Management* 24, no. 1 (1997): 97.

Hayuth, Y. *Intermodality: Concept and Practice*. London: Lloyds of London Press, 1987.

Hoyle, Brian S. and Richard Knowles. *Modern Transport Geography*. Edited on behalf of the Transport Geography Research Group of the Royal Geographical Society with the Institute of British Geographers. New York: Wiley, 1992.

Journal of Commerce (Malaysia), "New Malaysian Port Moves to Gain Singapore Business", 24 January 2001.

Kadir, Elias. "The Transformation of a Public Sector Transport Organization to a Private Entity: The KPM Experience". *Malaysian Transport* 3, no. 1 (1996): 20–34.

Mahoney, John H. *Intermodal Freight Transportation*. Westport, Conn.: Eno Foundation for Transportation, 1985.

New Straits Times, 21 July 1998, "Economics of Using Port Klang".

Phang, Datin."Port Klang: Its Development and Future Role". Paper presented at conference, Container Asia 1998, 10–12 November 1998, Sheraton Subang Hotel and Towers, Petaling Jaya, Malaysia.

Port of Thailand Authority (web site). www.lcp.pat.or.th Thailand: Laem Chabang Port.

PSA Annual Report 1998. PSA Ltd., 1999.

Shipping Times Online, 13 November 2000, "PTP Shifts Focus to Securing More Common Feeder Operators".

Shipping Times, 5 August 1997, "PSA Adopting Cost Reductions".

Shipping Times, 16 October 1997, "KL Shippers' Group to Promote Local Ports", p. 1.

Shipping Times, 12 January 2000,"Tanjung Pelepas offers similar level of services as PSA".

Shipping Times, 13 February 2001, "KL Gives Further Boost to Tanjung Pelepas Port".

Straits Times, 10 January 2001. Nicholas Fang, "PSA anchors year 2000 with record 17 m boxes moved", p. 10.

UNCTAD. *Port Marketing and the Challenge of the Third Generation Port*. United Nations, 1990.

3

Hub Ports

Recent trends in logistics management

In essence, any logistical operation involves the management of two distinct flows through the manufacturing organization: materials (physical products) and information. Each stage of the chain involves some element of transportation, warehousing and distribution.

In recent years, a number of changes have occurred in the realm of production as well as in the marketplace. These are caused by the changing geography of production nodes and the changing geography of markets: as evidenced by the greater demand for differentiated goods, product life cycles are becoming shorter, and consumer demands increasingly more unpredictable.

As a result, the twin requirements of efficiency and competitiveness in both production and sales have caused managers to recognize the importance of supplying the right goods to the right places at the right time for the right costs. Under this mode of thinking, the "Just-in-case" mode of storage and movement is beginning to be modified to JIT and lean operations. This naturally leads managers to rethink the strategic location and management of inventory and warehousing, the more careful selection and use of freight-forwarding services and port services, and the need for accurate and up-to-date information on cargo movements and sales. In addition, the traditional roles of transport and hub ports are given added significance.

Already, the world is witnessing two significant developments arising from the above-mentioned trends in logistics planning: less inventory holdings for high-value products and centralization of warehousing. International transportation and intermediate warehousing are taking centre stage. The trend is now towards exploiting cheaper sources of production and storage and using more efficient transhipment points for distribution of raw materials, intermediate products and finished goods for the global marketplace. This naturally leads to the next question, what are the ideal locations for hubs or hub ports? Marine transportation is predominantly the main source of transportation for time-insensitive cargo. This form of maritime trade has helped many countries to survive because of the revenue derived from their ports. The importance placed on hub ports cannot be undermined. Today, with greater globalization, this is even more apparent. As globalization brings trade between countries the importance of hub ports will surface, as most nations transport their goods by sea.

This chapter will start by explaining the concepts of hubbing and hub ports, and will identify some of characteristics and factors that make port a hub port. It will then examine four hub ports, Hong Kong, Singapore, Kaohsiung and Kobe, which have been chosen based on the number of TEUs handled. The characteristics of these four ports will be listed, and their recent and future developments examined, with emphasis on their efforts to stay ahead amidst keen competition and rapid growth in neighbouring ports. Finally, some generic strategies will be recommended to help the four hub ports to remain competitive, in the face of growing competition.

Hubbing in transportation

What exactly is hubbing? Put simply, industrial goods are brought to a central location (hub) and are either transhipped directly or are stored in warehouses before being distributed to their final destination. There is usually little physical transformation of these goods. Put in its proper perspective, this leads to the additional handling of goods and transit times, but provides cost- and time-sensitive users (Multinational Corporations) with enhanced flexibility (sea freight movement) and better economic returns (faster response to the market).

In logistics planning and management, the potential for hubbing arises in two situations in the flows of materials and products: transhipment hubbing (hubbing agents or freight forwarders), and planned distribution hubbing (hubbing agents or manufacturing companies).

Transhipment hubbing.   As manufacturing companies continue to be linked to a JIT, or close to JIT, system of inventory control and purchasing, they will continue to require timely transportation services at competitive prices. In reply, the freight forwarders have responded with an array of guaranteed-time delivery options. There is a good rationale for transhipment hubbing. A traditional reason for the use of transhipment is to manage the consolidation of activities. The argument for this is compelling, as the benefits of transhipment should bring about greater flexibility through lower costs, and reduce excess shipping capacity. Also, hubbing helps to promote the use of bigger vessels and higher frequencies (ship calls).

As such, the qualities of an ideal transhipment hub can be stated as follows:

1. Good geographical location in supply and demand regions
2. Efficient ground handling
3. Unpacking/reconsolidation activities by freight forwarders to ensure of maximum convenience
4. Good and stable supply of sea services
5. Adequate and well-managed ancillary services and infrastructure.

Planned-distribution hubbing.   Two types of distribution hubbing currently exist, planned-distribution hubbing and "importer-exporter" hubbing. In this section, we focus on planned-distribution hubbing. One reason for this is the proliferation of Multinational Corporations in Southeast and East Asia. In the 1970s, branch plants were restricted to a few countries. In the 1980s and a good part of the 1990s, there was greater fragmentation and specialization of individual tasks, resulting in more branch plants in Southeast Asia which evolved into a growing market for a variety of finished products.

In terms of the evolution of the hub-and-spoke distribution method of doing business, many changes have taken place. Firstly, there has been greater centralization of warehousing and distribution of important inputs and products. Secondly, multinationals were demanding greater transit-time flexibility and lower costs in distribution where possible. As a result, the management of logistical functions in planned-distribution hubbing also evolved. First, some multinationals started to have their own warehouses, and appointed forwarders for transportation. Next, they started to seek greater outsourcing of the warehousing function to public warehousing companies and third party providers. Some qualities of an ideal hub for planned distribution have included:

1. Strong EDI capabilities
2. Public sector agencies or state authorities who are willing to work in cooperation with distribution companies to streamline operations (such as trade facilitation)
3. Suitable manpower and space for warehousing at low costs
4. Sufficient direct traffic flow to supplement re-export traffic (distribution companies need diversified sources of demand)
5. An efficient integrated transportation system, as international distribution usually involves multi-modal transport.

Some characteristics of hub ports

Hub ports work on the principle that small fleets of fast and large line-haul vessels call on only main ports at each end of the globe or strategic locations. The hub ports feed the smaller regional ports using a small fleet of feeder vessels (smaller vessels).

This keeps the ratio of port time versus sea time low, and also gives a good transit time between main ports. From this rationale, it can be seen that hub ports are basically transhipment points whereby containers are transferred from feeder vessels to storage in a terminal and then onto large long-line-haul vessels. Some of the benefits of good hub ports can be argued as follows.

Hub ports reduce the complexity of shipping services.   For example, suppose there are ten ports in Asia trading with ten ports in Europe. In an extreme scenario, there would be direct calls between each pair of ports and resulting in 100 complex combinations of port pairs requiring 100 individual shipping services. With a hub port, this number could be cut down to 20, with the ten ports on each side calling at the hub (Leong 1997). This would constitute a complexity reduction of five times.

Hub ports enable economies of scale.   Consolidation of containers at hub ports enables large vessels to be completely filled or almost fully utilized. Thus, large ocean-going vessels are able to minimize the number of port calls. Economies are achieved as relatively more containers are transported on the large vessels over a longer distance. Over the shorter distances between the feeder ports and the hubs, cheaper, faster and smaller vessels are used. This ensures that the vessels are fully utilized on these shorter routes, as the flow of traffic is not enough to require large vessels. For example, containers travelling to Europe from Asia will be consolidated at Singapore by small feeder vessels. In this way, a large long-line vessel will carry these containers to Rotterdam, where the containers will be distributed to different European countries. The use of large vessels, which are needed for long-line hauls, is minimized and fully utilized, and the cost per container shipped is reduced, underscoring scale economies. Also, with fewer ships embarking on long trips, the major sea lanes of the world are less congested.

Hub ports provide a wider shipping selection, fast transit time and high shipping frequency.   In Singapore, a container may be connected to 700 destinations via 130 shipping lines. Every week, 22 ships depart for Europe, 30 for Japan and 14 for North America. About 100 feeder vessels distribute cargo to and consolidate cargo from regional ports. Shippers can adopt close to JIT manufacturing to reduce inventory cost and achieve shorter time-to-market for their products. For example, a shipper in Sydney has only a weekly sailing frequency if he wants to ship his containers to Rotterdam directly, as there is only one ship per week. It would therefore, take his containers 40 days to reach the destination. For about the same freight rate he pays for direct shipping, the shipper can tranship his containers via Singapore to Rotterdam in about 35 days. In addition, he enjoys more sailing frequencies, as there are 6 sailings a week from Sydney to Singapore and 21 sailings from Singapore to Rotterdam. This translates into greater flexibility for production and loading schedules and longer shut-out times.

The whole network of ports can benefit from strategic hub arrangements. In a world in which only direct shipping among ports were available, each port would receive cargo directly from other ports. The berth capacity that each port would have to provide for direct shipment would be tremendous. With transhipment, each port needs only to provide for ships calling from the hub ports. This helps to reduce unnecessary and expensive investment in berths and other port facilities.

Factors required to create a hub port

Location.   Ports which are located along the main trade routes, or routes with minimum deviations and surrounded by industrialized regions, are considered natural hubs. They must also have a natural well-dredged harbour with channels and alongside drafts able to accommodate large vessels under all tidal conditions (that is, deep-water berths).

Capability.   Hub ports must have the capability to minimize the turnaround time of vessels. They should have state-of-the-art equipment, harmonized procedures with minimum documentation, a high level of computerization and technological developments in their operating systems and communications link-ups with all parties, a sensible organizational structure for effective operation control, and a good customer relations culture (Idris 1996).

Safe environment.   There must be well-established and well-organized port security and policing functions, port safety and dangerous cargo functions, and harmonious industrial relations with the harbour unions.

Conducive commercial environment.   Hub port rates and charges must be attractive, transparent, sensible, simplified and flexible. A strong commercial or marketing department manned by staff who are conversant with terminal operations and procedures as well as the ability to maintain friendly relations must back the application of these rates and charges. This will enable the port to attract large captive cargo and allay fears of over-investment.

Free commercial (trade) zones.   These zones are provided for distribution, consolidation, value-added and re-export services to minimize transit and wait times.

Ancillary services.   Additional services such as telecommunications, water supplies, ship repairs, waste disposal and medical services must be provided.

Port-related government agencies and commercial services.   Services such as port regulatory authorities, customs, immigration, health, agriculture, veterinaries, banking, insurance and surveyors must be available to efficiently and intelligently serve port users 24-hours a day, 7 days a week.

We now explore some of the regional hub ports in ASEAN and East Asia: Hong Kong, Singapore, Kaohsiung and Kobe.

Hong Kong

Hong Kong was the world's busiest container port in 1997 and has held this position intermittently since 1992. Located at the mouth of the Pearl River Delta, it has become the gateway to China ever since the opening up of China's economy, and it has developed into a major international port for South China and much of the rest of the country. About 90 per cent of the cargo to and from southern China passes through Hong Kong.

Port facilities in Hong Kong include 6,059 metres of quays at Kwai Chung and 8 container terminals at Stonecutters Bay that can accommodate up to 19 third-generation container ships simultaneously. These container terminals have a combined capacity of 11.5 million TEUs and handle about two-thirds of Hong Kong's total throughput. In addition, there are 7,742 m of quays at public cargo working areas and 61 mooring buoys for ocean-going vessels.

There are three modes of operation at the Port of Hong Kong: container terminal, mid-stream and river-trade operations. In 1997, the Port of Hong Kong handled a total of 14.5 million TEUs. Some 1.9 million TEUs were handled by river-trade operators for vessels making use of the numerous waterways in the Pearl River Delta area to transport cargo to and from Guangdong, China. More than one-fifth of the container throughput is handled through mid-stream operators for small- and medium-sized ships engaging in intra-Asian trade. The rest of the container throughput is handled by container terminal operators for ocean-going vessels.

Ship turnaround performance in the Port of Hong Kong is among the best in Asia. Container ships at terminal berths are routinely turned around in 10 hours or less, while conventional vessels working cargo at buoys are in port for only 1.9 days on average (Thompson 1998).

Hong Kong is the only major international port in the world which is fully privatized. The private sector finances, builds, owns and operates new terminals in response to market demand. This policy enables Hong Kong to take advantage of the commercial skills and flexibility of private operators and to keep bureaucratic red tape to a minimum. The government provides the necessary back-up land, navigation channels, infrastructure and utilities.

Hong Kong does not have a port authority; the Marine Department of the Hong Kong Special Administrative Region is responsible for the day-to-day administration of the port. However, there is also a Port Development Board, which recommends strategies for creating new port facilities and coordinates government and private sector involvement in their development. The Board acts as a focal point for ideas and opinions expressed by port operators and anyone affected by port expansion.

Recent and future developments

To ensure that facilities match demand, the Port Development Board produces port cargo forecasts biannually. In February 1998, this forecast projected that the throughput of the Hong Kong container port will grow at an average rate of 5.8 per cent up to 2006 and 3.1 per cent thereafter until 2016. In terms of container numbers, the throughput is expected to increase from 14.5 million TEUs in 1997 to 24 million TEUs in 2006 and 33 million TEUs in 2016 (World Reporter 1998).

Given this projection, plans have been made to accommodate future port needs, as failure to provide adequate facilities on time would result in port congestion and severe economic losses. The new Container Terminal 9 will have six berths, with the first scheduled to become operational by the end of 2001. The remaining berths will come into operation at five- to six-month intervals. The whole terminal is expected to be ready by 2004, with a design capacity of 2.6 million TEUs. However, this terminal on Tsing Yi Island will be the last terminal in the Kwai Chung area.

Consideration has been made to develop Container Terminals 10 and 11. When completed, these two terminals at Lantau Port will have a total capacity equal to that of Rotterdam. A review of port operations is carried out every quarter and a comprehensive review of port needs, every two years. Decisions related to Container Terminals 10 and 11 will be made at the next comprehensive review at around 2002.

To improve the efficiency of river-trade operations, lower the cost of transporting containers between Hong Kong and the Pearl River Delta, and relieve congestion on the road system, a river-trade terminal has been built in West Tuen Mun. The terminal is designed to consolidate containers coming down from the Pearl River Delta ports before feeding them to the Kwai Chung container terminals or mid-stream operators. The new terminal has a design capacity to handle 1.3 million TEUs of river-trade cargo each year.

Competition

Although the Port of Hong Kong has virtually no competition for southern Chinese cargo, it faces fierce rivalry for cargo from other parts of China. As a result, it posted growth of only 7 per cent in 1996 and 8 per cent in 1997, a contrast from the double-digit increases in preceding years. The Port of Hong Kong had faced virtually no competition until recently. In the past several years, there has been widespread port development in the Pearl River Delta that is gaining momentum each year. The Shenzhen ports together handled 1.1 million TEUs in 1997 — about 8 per cent of Hong Kong's throughput (Penfold 1997).

In addition, Korea has also begun to handle transhipment cargo from northern and eastern China. However, Kobe, which has always handled large volumes of northern and eastern Chinese transhipment cargo, is less of a concern. As Kobe is considered very expensive in the shipping world, it is not likely to attract transhipment cargo from Hong Kong.

Future outlook

The Port of Hong Kong will remain the main international gateway for southern China. However, the proportion of southern Chinese cargo shipped through Hong Kong is forecast to drop from the current 90 per cent share to roughly 50 per cent in the next decade, with the rest handled by Yantian, Shekou and the other mainland ports. Despite this, the port will continue to grow due to the increasing export cargo from South China. It has been forecast that Hong Kong's total container throughput will increase from 63 per cent in 1996 to 76 per cent in 2016.

The likelihood of Hong Kong remaining the gateway to the whole of China is not great. The resumption of direct trade between China and Taiwan, and the fast development of China's other ports is likely to erode demand for the port's services. Presently, only foreign-registered vessels to and from two southern Chinese ports, Xiamen and Fuzhou, are allowed transhipment of goods through Kaohsiung. However, future liberalization of direct shipping links between China and Taiwan will take business away from Hong Kong. It is anticipated that about 80–90 per cent of the cargo (about one million TEUs) which is currently shipped between China and Taiwan via Hong Kong will be affected. In addition, further growth of the other Chinese ports will also erode the attractiveness of Hong Kong.

Singapore

The Port of Singapore comprises six terminals accommodating all types of vessels — container ships, bulk carriers, cargo freighters, coasters, lighters and passenger liners. Depending on their cargo, these vessels will either call at the oil terminals run by the petroleum companies or the terminals run by the PSA Corporation and the Jurong Town Corporation (JTC). The PSA operates the terminals at Brani, Keppel, Pasir Panjang, Sembawang and Tanjung Pagar, which deal in container and conventional cargo. Jurong Port, which handles conventional and bulk cargo, comes under the purview of the JTC. (See also the profile of the Port of Singapore given in Chapter 2.)

Singapore as a transhipment hub

Singapore has strong sea port facilities which are adequate, modern and well-integrated, making it a renowned 24-hour one-stop sea cargo service centre. There is also a good support of ancillary services and the telecommunications infrastructure is adequate. The supply of sea services is also adequate, as Singapore is served by many international scheduled carriers, many of which provide full-freighter services.

Government policy towards freight-forwarding operations is friendly. An open-door policy towards foreign forwarding companies has always been in place and the relevant public sector agencies have taken great pains to ensure that adequate facilities are available in the FTZ. The objective is to turn Singapore into a sea–air transhipment centre.

Singapore as a planned-distribution hub

To help transform Singapore into a logistics distribution hub, the government has endeavoured to ensure that well-developed infrastructure and services are present. These are found in the state-of-the-art communications systems, excellent banking and financial services, modern port facilities, comprehensive road networks, a skilled, disciplined labour force and pro-business policies. Some of these policies and incentives include schemes for distribution activities, OHQ and BHQ status.

Trade and businesses are also helping to turn Singapore into a distribution hub. For a start, Singapore has a sufficiently high level of regional demand to supplement intra-ASEAN container flows. Many multinationals located in Singapore are characterized by significant outsourcing and many logistics distribution companies are setting up base in Singapore. In distribution management, the need for coordination extends from decisions on sources of supply of raw materials and components, through manufacturing and assembly to the customer. Towards this end, EDI and web-based systems have become tools of significant value. Manufacturing and distribution companies have their own systems, but EDI ties between these distribution agents and airlines, shipping lines, customs and trade authorities are needed at a hub. In the case of the Port of Singapore, there are good EDI systems in place, such as TradeNet and PortNet.

Recent and future developments

To pre-empt competition, Singapore has been increasing its infrastructure investments. The PSA recently built a 26-berth terminal in Pasir Panjang in the western part of Singapore, at a cost of S$7 billion. The terminal employs new-generation quay cranes that can handle the largest ships in the world (18-container width) and a remote-controlled bridge crane that can increase berth capacity by up to one-third. The first four berths begun operations in 1998. When completed, the terminal will have a handling capacity of at least 18 million TEUs, making it Southeast Asia's largest container facility.

Singapore recently increased its budget threefold to S$1.12 billion. Part of this sum went into FastConnect II, an updated version of the port's cargo-information system targeted at the key transhipment business. The use of the system has reduced the average time containers stay in the port to an average of 4.0 days, compared with 4.65 days in 1995. This translates into an increase in the PSA's handling capacity, as more containers can be stored in its yards at any given time. Shipping lines also enjoy faster turnaround times as a result of tighter connections. The average turnaround has improved from 14.7 hours to 11.3 hours during the same period. A third-generation container vessel is serviced at an average rate of 84 containers per ship hour. About 95 per cent of vessels are berthed upon arrival, and more than 50 per cent of containers are transhipped within three days.

The PSA is hoping to gain further efficiency through privatization and greater automation. The use of automated guided vehicles will become operational by the year 2004. In addition, the PSA itself has streamlined its internal organization, cut rates and nailed down new long-term contracts.

Competition

Singapore is experiencing competition from other regional ports, with Tanjung Priok, Port Klang, Tanjung Pelepas and Laem Chabang all handling containers as their principal cargo. In addition, as discussed in the previous chapter, Port Klang, Manila and Laem Chabang have become ports of call for some mainline vessels. Although the combined throughput of the ports of

Malaysia, Thailand and all the other Southeast Asian nations put together is only a fraction of Singapore's annual traffic, each additional box these ports handle is one taken away from Singapore.

Such developments offer shipping lines good alternatives, especially when disputes break out over rates. In 1996, when the PSA imposed a 10 per cent increase in terminal fees several companies, including APL and Taiwan's Evergreen Marine Corporation, threatened to switch their transhipment bases to Batam. The potential loss prompted the PSA to scale back the increase, suggesting the elasticity of demand.

Future outlook

Despite the emergence of competitive ports elsewhere in Southeast Asia, Singapore should remain the major transhipment port for this region. Though some direct long-haul services to other regional ports have been established and are increasing in number, the very largest vessels can still only be accommodated by Singapore.

Kaohsiung

Kaohsiung Harbour is the largest international harbour in Taiwan (the Republic of China). It is situated on Taiwan's southwestern coast, and is the pivot point at the intersection between the Taiwan Strait and the Bashi Strait. It boasts a spreading harbour, expansive hinterland and a mild climate. Off the sea, it has a narrow and long sandbar which forms the natural breakwater.

Kaohsiung is an international transporting centre and pivotal harbour. It is also used as a manufacturing and distribution base for re-exported and value-added goods. In addition, it is a multi-functional international harbour and a major harbour of container transportation in Taiwan. It is also the largest importing harbour of liquid and bulk cargo in south Taiwan.

Recent and future developments

Kaohsiung was the top-ranked container throughput port before 1980. However, the situation changed due to China's opening up to the western world and the development of the special economic zones along its coast. Kaohsiung is now used mainly used as a transhipment port for US products into the Asian market.

Kaohsiung has been growing steadily over the years. Its traffic volume has increased steadily and reached more than 4.5 million TEUs in 1993. With Taiwan trying to establish direct shipping links with China, there could even be more areas into which Kaohsiung can expand in the future.

Kaohsiung has plans to become a major transhipment hub. Major projects to support Kaohsiung as a hub port, such as the expansion of the international airport and the construction of highways, are being undertaken. There are also plans for the development of an inter-modal container-rail system to link the Port of Kaohsiung with the Port of Taichung. Besides all these, there are also plans to expand the harbour area and the port itself. The harbour area will be re-adjusted to serve as an entertainment spot for residents of Kaohsiung, making the best use of existing harbour resources and establishing a multifunctional harbour. A new turning basin will be built and two existing buoys removed. The depth of the present turning basin will also be increased. The dock will be moved and expanded, and the wharves reconstructed. Chienchen Fishing Harbour will also be reconstructed into a container terminal. In addition, an offshore container terminal and harbour administration area will be constructed, and the Talin Commercial Harbour will see the construction of a new wharf.

Kaohsiung Harbour also intends to use more IT. It plans to connect the Harbour Service Network by computer, to automate its customs and warehousing services and to computerize the processing of official documents. In addition, it hopes to establish a vessel-transportation management system to help increase capacity and the efficiency of cargo services on certain water areas, as well as to maintain order and ensure safety.

Competition

Competition comes mainly from China and Hong Kong. As China is keen to develop its ports, shippers could just ship direct to the Chinese ports instead of passing through Kaohsiung. Also, with Hong Kong under Chinese rule, shippers might prefer to use Hong Kong as a transhipment port for goods bound for the mainland. Further, it would be very difficult for Kaohsiung to overtake Singapore and/or Hong Kong as the leading transhipment port, as the latter are already well established and more efficient than Kaohsiung. Kaohsiung's niche is therefore to concentrate on the transhipment of North American goods to Asia and compete with the Korean and Japanese ports.

Future outlook

With the possibility of direct shipping between Taiwan and mainland China, Kaohsiung cannot aspire to become a major transhipment hub without the support of the large Chinese market.

Strategies for hub ports to remain competitive

Due to the many uncertainties such as economic fluctuations, government regulations, the instability of political instability and business agendas, and the future growth rates of the global economy — affecting the three hub ports discussed thus far, it is not wise to recommend specific strategies for each port. However, we have taken the approach of recommending some generic strategies that the ports can adopt to stay competitive. These strategies are as follows:

Providing port infrastructure. Container terminals will have to upgrade or risk limiting their ability to accommodate bigger ships, as shipping lines will be selective in their choice of port calls in order to optimize their asset deployment. For instance, channels and berths will have to be dredged deeper to accommodate the new, larger vessels, and quay cranes will have to be expanded as the beam of these super-tankers increases from 13 rows across 4,000 TEUs to 17 rows across 6,000 TEUs.

Operational performances. Port operations must be geared to control terminal handling costs in order to help shipping lines reduce their operating costs. However, what matters most will be not low prices, but lowest *overall cost* in the entire chain and *value-for-money* services to maximize returns.

The importance of a hub port to its customers will be judged on its ability to cater for *speed* (vessel turnaround time has to be improved to reduce port time and minimize round voyage time); and *service reliability* (port operators must help liners meet their sailing time schedules). To meet these new challenges, traditional work processes must be reengineered to make way for new ones.

Information technology. The use of technology will allow ports to increase the productivity of their resources and add value to their customers through the streamlining of operations (Fu 1997). IT can be used to:

1. Increase efficiency. IT systems can be used to handle heavier workloads and more complicated plans without compromizing efficiency and accuracy. Planning lead-time can also be reduced so that port operations can respond to dynamic changes quickly.
2. Online information access. Information access will provide that extra edge for competing in the global marketplace. Port operators can provide their customers with online and easy-to-access real-time information, such as EDI on the status of vessels or containers. Unproductive work can be eliminated, as plans and documents are sent electronically.
3. Automation. IT will form the foundation for automating port operations, such as using AGVs.

Human resources. Port operators need to lay greater emphasis on the skilled personnel required to integrate and streamline operations (Olsen 1997). Many critically important port management activities are carried out not by state-of-the-art computerized robots but by well-qualified and suitably trained individuals who can think and react to scenarios which have no precedence.

Shippers' port selection factors. Port operators must be customer-oriented — that is, they must be aware of and cater to customer needs. Some of the factors which Murphy et al. (1992) determined as being important to shippers when selecting ports are:

1. Loading and unloading facilities for large and/or odd-sized freight
2. Allowance for large-volume shipments
3. Acceptance of/Allowance for low freight handling shipments
4. Low frequency of loss and damage
5. Availability of equipment
6. Convenient pickup and delivery times
7. Provision of information concerning shipments
8. Assistance in claims handling offered
9. Flexibility in meeting special handling requirements.

Future regional hubs

More regions are expected to be significant players in the transhipment stakes, although Southeast Asia will also account for an increased share of the market — as much as one third of all activity by the year 2005. Expected future candidates for the role of transhipment hub in Southeast Asia include Tanjung Pelepas, Port Klang, and Laem Chabang.

Port of Tanjung Pelepas

Despite the uncertainty of the potential of this port, as it is a somewhat unknown entity at the moment, it seems that Tanjung Pelepas is likely to pose the biggest threat to the port of Singapore's position as the premier transhipment hub in the region. One major selling point of the port is that it is new, flexible, has state-of-the-art facilities, good financial backing, room to

TABLE 3.1
Handling Charges Per Container,[a] 1999

	Port Klang		Singapore		Laem	Chabang	Tanjung Pelepas[b]	
	20 ft	40 ft	20 ft	40 ft	20 ft	40 ft	20 ft	40 ft
FCL	RM190 (US$50)	RM285 (US$75)	S$270 (US$155)	S$382 (US$220)	THB972 (US$23)	THB1462 (US$34)	S$189 (US$109)	S$267 (US$154)
LCL	RM330 (US$87)	RM490 (US$129)	S$565 (US$325)	S$786 (US$452)	THB2500 (US$58)	THB3995 (US$93)	S$395 (US$227)	S$550 (US$316)
Transhipment	RM160 (US$42)	RM240 (US$63)	S$174 (US$100)	S$252 (US$145)	THB462 (US$11)	THB697 (US$16)	S$121 (US$70)	S$176 (US$101)

Notes: [a] Tanjung Pelepas's rates are calculated at an estimated of 70 per cent of Singapore's rates as according to industry estimates.
[b] Exchange rates used are US$1 = S$1.74, US$1 = RM3.8 and US$1 = THB42.8.

Source: *Fairplay Port Guide 1999/2000.*

expand, the ability to cater to post-Panamax vessels, warehousing facilities, an IT system, hinterland links and an initial base cargo. The port is also willing to offer dedicated berths to certain customers, which the port of Singapore currently does not provide.

Another factor is its close proximity (20 km at the most) to the natural beneficial geographical location which Singapore enjoys and which contributes to its success.

The recent move of Maersk-Sealand to Tanjung Pelepas has offered cargo owners the alternative of shipping their cargo to a port where the costs are much lower, compared to the cost structures at the Port of Singapore. Table 3.1 shows that Tanjung Pelepas is estimated to charge about 30 per cent less than Singapore. Tanjung Pelepas has already managed to capture 1.8 million TEUs from Singapore, more than 10 per cent of Singapore's throughput in 1999 (*Investors Digest* 2000).

Port Klang

Although the volume of cargo generated at Port Klang lags behind that of the port of Singapore, it has consistently experienced spectacular growth rates (except for during the crisis years 1997–98) averaging 20 per cent (see Figure 3.1). This compares favourably with the growth rates experienced by the port of Singapore.

FIGURE 3.1
Growth Rate of Containers Handled

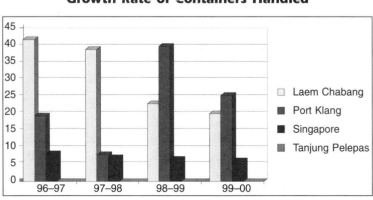

Port efficiency as measured in terms of crane productivity has also improved rapidly. As Figure 3.2 shows, Port Klang experienced double-digit growth in terms of crane productivity, compared with Singapore's 6 per cent, in 1999.

FIGURE 3.2
Crane Productivity
(TEUs Per Crane Hour)

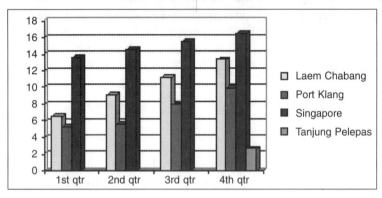

Notes: Total crane hours = no. of cranes × 365 × 24

Crane productivity = no. of TEUs ÷ no. of crane hours.

The cranes are used 24 hours a day at all ports.

Cranes used are quay cranes, ship–shore cranes and mobile cranes. Productivity figures are based on the current number in use.

Total relevant cranes for each port: Laem Chabang 18, Port Klang 37, Singapore 118, Tanjung Pelepas 18.

Source: Computed from official web sites, newspapers and *Fairplay Port Guide* 1999/2000.

Laem Chabang

As shown in Figure 3.2, the Port of Laem Chabang has continuously improved crane productivity and is catching up with the port of Singapore. A study by the Research and Business Services Centre at Chulalongkorn University found that shipping-line efficiency at the port is comparable to that of other ports in the region except for Singapore (Port Authority of Thailand 1999).

Given its strategic location (its proximity to the rest of Indochina) this port may become a transhipment hub for cargo originating from or bound for Indochina. Since it would take an estimated two and a half day increase in the amount of time for ships taking the Straits of Malacca route to call at the Port of Laem Chabang, this port would probably not be in a position to take much of the transhipment business in the future. This, however, could change if the Kra canal project, which has been in the pipeline for many years, goes ahead (*The Straits Times* 2001). This project, which involves digging an international waterway through the Kra Isthmus in the southern region of Thailand, would serve as a faster alternative international shipping route linking Europe and the Far East. Several foreign investors have shown interest in funding the project, which is said to have enjoyed good support from Japan's global infrastructure fund.

Conclusion

The role of hub ports is crucial, as they enable efficiency and offer greater value for money. Their stature will only grow as the amount of goods shipped increases and new improvements in ship technology enable bigger, faster and more efficient ships. Thus, it can be envisaged that the present four hub ports in Asia are likely to face competition from emerging transhipment ports and direct ports-of-call. The strategies presented can only enable the ports to compete more effectively and help them to maintain their status quo. Despite all the challenges and threats faced by the four ports, they will continue to remain the key players in the region and the world-at-large. However, they should not grow complacent, but strive instead to maintain their current status and position, as they will be the ultimate beneficiaries in the long run.

References

Fu, Grace. "The Future of Singapore Port — Strategies to Remain Competitive". Paper presented at Conference, Ports Asia 1997, 23–25 July 1997.

Idris, B.M. "Developing a port's transhipment activities". *Container Asia '96*.

Leong, T.Y. "Do Transhipment hubs create value?". *Port View*, February/ March 1997, pp. 14–16.

Murphy, P., J.M. Daly, and D.R. Dalenberg. "Port Selection Criteria: An Application of a Transportation Framework". *Logistics and Transportation Review* 28, no. 3 (1992): 237–56.

Olsen, Jens-Erik. "Ports from a Shipowner's Point of View". Paper presented at conference, Ports Asia 1997, 23–25 July 1997.

Penfold, Andrew. "Regional Container Traffic Growth Expectations — What are the implications for port facilities planning in Asia?", Ports *Asia 1997*.

Thompson. Paper presented at forum, Asian Ports: Competition or Co-operation — Independence or Interdependence, 25 March 1998. Web reference: <www.info.gov.hk/mardep/port/port.htm>.

World Reporter, "Hong Kong cuts 1998 container throughput growth forecast to 3–5 per cent from 5–6 per cent", 12 February 1998.

World Reporter (TM), "Bold plans to attract cargo", 28 January 1999.

Hong Kong's Port Development, www.info.gov.hk/mardep/.

<www.singapore.inc.com/psa.html> and <http://www.mpa.gov.sg/-homepage/theport.html>.

4

Forecast of Container Volumes and Patterns of Transhipment

The previous chapters were mainly concerned with the implications of the changing port environment on port operations and the various development policies and strategies adopted by major ports in the region. This chapter will try to evaluate the future container market and business opportunities that are likely to face the ports in the region. This is important so that ports in the region can plan appropriately and thus be able to take advantage of these opportunities.

Past trends in world container volumes

The volume of container cargo handled by the container ports in the world grew on average by 9 per cent per annum in the period 1990–98. However, due to the rapid rise in transhipment volumes through the key hub ports, the growth rate for containerized trade is slightly lower than the growth of containers handled at ports. Containerized trade grew on average by around 7 per cent over the same period, whereas the average growth in total trade tonnage was only 2.8 per cent (Avery 2000). Figure 4.1 illustrates this growth, showing a consistent

FIGURE 4.1

Total World Port Volumes, 1983–98

(Million TEUs)

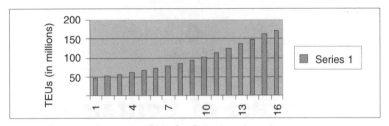

Source: Container International Yearbook (various issues).

increase despite the Asian crisis from roughly 46 million TEUs in 1983 to 172 million TEUs in 1998.

This robust growth in container traffic has been driven by the following major factors: world economic growth, the continued rise in world trade and the growing industrialization of developing countries.

When there is an increase in economic activity, as manifested in increased gross national output, there is an increase in imports and thus in world trade. Over the past decade the world has consistently been growing. Moreover, the world economy has become increasingly dependent on trade, with each major regional trading grouping rapidly accelerating the level of goods transferred both between economies in the region and between the major trading blocs. For example, the formation of the EU and of the North American Free Trade Area has resulted in greater amounts of goods traded in the world, as they have spurred the world towards multilateralism. Containerization has also facilitated the transfer of finished goods between nations. As developing nations continue to industrialize, demand for containers will grow.

Future world container volumes

Ocean Shipping Consultants (1999) has provided forecasts for container volumes on a global and regional basis up to the year 2012 under optimistic and pessimistic scenarios. These forecasts are summarized in Table 4.1.

TABLE 4.1
Forecast World Container Port Demand to 2012
(Million TEUs)

	1997	1998	2000	2004-I	2004-II	2008-I	2008-II	2012-I	2012-II
North & West Europe	27.12	29.37	32.85	41.15	39.70	49.01	46.39	57.07	53.21
Mediterranean	16.26	18.71	22.27	28.46	25.92	36.19	32.58	43.61	37.30
Middle East	6.63	7.19	8.60	12.91	11.65	16.74	14.90	20.90	19.10
Indian Sub-Continent	4.43	4.71	5.60	7.50	6.95	10.50	9.75	12.20	11.10
Northeast Asia	19.31	19.86	22.20	30.52	26.62	39.61	32.86	48.50	38.68
China Port Region	29.21	31.56	37.90	51.40	45.00	66.50	54.50	83.85	67.97
Southeast Asia	26.83	27.59	33.55	55.70	47.59	76.50	61.25	105.11	85.00
North America	24.77	26.81	29.84	37.87	35.50	48.32	45.15	57.73	52.75
Central America & Caribbean	7.96	9.08	10.74	15.08	13.55	20.13	17.59	24.54	21.30
South America	4.92	5.20	6.44	9.31	8.00	12.91	11.40	16.40	14.90
Australasia	3.81	4.09	4.45	5.43	5.18	6.77	6.24	8.44	7.47
Africa	3.52	3.68	4.13	6.04	5.82	8.87	7.23	12.75	9.00
Total	174.75	187.75	218.57	301.37	271.48	392.05	339.84	491.10	417.78

TABLE 4.1 (continued)

	1997	1998	2000	2004-I	2004-II	2008-I	2008-II	2012-I	2012-II
Percentage									
North & West Europe	15.52	15.64	15.03	13.65	14.62	12.50	13.65	11.62	12.74
Mediterranean	9.30	9.96	10.19	9.44	9.55	9.23	9.59	8.88	8.93
Middle East	3.79	3.83	3.93	4.28	4.29	4.27	4.38	4.26	4.57
Indian Sub-Continent	2.54	2.51	2.56	2.49	2.56	2.68	2.87	2.48	2.66
Northeast Asia	11.05	10.57	10.16	10.13	9.81	10.10	9.67	9.88	9.26
China Port Region	16.71	16.80	17.34	17.06	16.58	16.96	16.04	17.07	16.27
Southeast Asia	15.35	14.69	15.35	18.48	17.53	19.51	18.02	21.40	20.35
North America	14.18	14.27	13.65	12.57	13.08	12.32	13.29	11.76	12.63
Central America & Caribbean	4.55	4.83	4.91	5.00	4.99	5.13	5.18	5.00	5.10
South America	2.81	2.77	2.95	3.09	2.95	3.29	3.35	3.34	3.57
Australasia	2.18	2.18	2.04	1.80	1.91	1.73	1.84	1.72	1.79
Africa	2.01	1.96	1.89	2.00	2.14	2.26	2.13	2.60	2.15
Total	100.00	100.00	100.00	100.00	100.00	100.00	100.00	100.00	100.00

I refers to the optimistic scenario; II refers to the pessimistic scenario.
Source: *Ocean Shipping Consultants* (1999) p. 33.

Under the optimistic scenario, total demand is expected to grow by 125 per cent between 2000 and 2012 to a total of 491 million TEUs in 2012, based on the following assumptions:

1. OECD economic growth at the upper end of long-range forecasts
2. Successful deregulation, restructuring and revitalization of the Japanese economy, resulting in a closer balance in its trade flow
3. Political stability and economic expansion in China
4. Renewed economic and currency stability in the Asian region
5. Stability of the European Monetary Union (EMU)
6. Successful management of the U.S. economic slowdown
7. Continuing deregulation and privatization in Latin America
8. Political stabilization of the Middle East continuing, thus renewing confidence in increasing inward investment
9. Economic liberalization progress in India and Pakistan
10. Sub-Saharan African recovery centred on continued confidence, investment and growth in the South African economy and the continued implementation of market-oriented reforms and the policies of structural changes elsewhere.

Under the pessimistic scenario, total demand will increase by only around 91 per cent to about 417 million TEUs by 2012, under the realization of slowdown in growth and other adverse economic conditions as follows:

1. OECD economic growth at the lower end of long-range forecasts
2. Further stagnation in the Japanese economy
3. Periods of economic uncertainty (including devaluation) in China
4. Failure to follow through with polices of macroeconomic and structural adjustment in Asia.
5. Difficulties in adjusting to the European Monetary Union
6. Difficulties with the U.S. economic slowdown and stock market uncertainty.
7. Patchy and incomplete deregulation in Latin America

8. Middle East
9. Slower pace of economic restructuring in India
10. Lack of confidence, investment and growth in South Africa

Regional forecasts

The East and Southeast Asian economies have been at the forefront of world container trade growth since the mid-1980s. Although the currency crisis affected these countries adversely, it seems that the worst effects have already passed and there is expectation of a return to the kind of steady growth that had been noted prior to 1997. Despite the crisis, Asian markets still topped the charts for container trade, with a total of some 79.03 million TEUs in 1998, as can be seen in Table 4.2. This is more than 40 per cent of the total world container trade. Despite the varying degrees of economic growth faced by different regions, the general trend is expected to be one of rapid growth. In the most optimistic scenario, growth is expected to be almost 9 per cent each year, reaching 237.46 million TEUs in 2012. Even under a pessimistic outlook, where export-oriented regional economies such as that of Singapore are adversely affected, growth is still expected to grow around 6 per cent every year to reach more than double its current amount to 191.65 million TEUs in 2012.

In Southeast Asia, where containerization is already more established, despite the initial effects of the currency crisis (exposing the weaker regional industries and prompting a very significant restructuring which will benefit the region in the future), the rate of growth is expected to be very strong, capturing up to 20 per cent of the total world container trade. Although the Southeast Asian market is enlarging its share of world demand, Singapore, which traditionally captures a large share of the market, is forecasted to lose its dominance in the Southeast Asian market (see Table 4.2). This is because its share of container trade in the region is expected to be eroded, as port development elsewhere in the region (such as at Tanjung Pelepas) accelerates. Despite this setback, Singapore is still expected capture more than one third of the Southeast Asian container trade, which is expected to reach more than 30 million TEUs in throughput under

TABLE 4.2
Forecast East Asian Container Port Demand by Region
(Million TEUs)

	1997	1998	2000	2004-I	2004-II	2008-I	2008-II	2012-I	2012-II
Japan	10.89	10.78	11.35	13.85	12.15	15.75	13.22	17.85	14.51
South Korea	5.86	5.93	6.45	8.94	7.47	11.26	9.55	13.50	11.62
Northeast China	2.64	3.03	4.25	7.53	6.85	12.35	9.89	16.85	12.30
Russia	0.10	0.12	0.15	0.20	0.15	0.25	0.20	0.30	0.25
Northeast Asia	19.31	19.86	22.20	30.52	26.62	39.61	32.86	48.50	38.68
Hong Kong	14.54	14.69	16.15	18.95	17.90	22.05	19.20	25.80	21.90
Taiwan	8.48	8.82	9.90	13.21	12.85	17.00	15.75	20.80	18.65
South & East China	6.19	8.06	11.85	19.24	14.25	27.45	19.55	37.25	27.42
China Port Region	29.21	31.57	37.90	51.40	45.00	66.50	54.50	83.85	67.97
Singapore	14.12	15.10	16.95	23.95	21.70	26.50	23.25	36.40	31.50
Philippines	3.05	2.88	3.85	7.40	6.15	10.95	8.25	15.20	12.50
Indonesia	3.18	2.94	3.50	6.90	4.70	10.35	6.50	14.25	9.15
Malaysia	3.02	3.08	3.85	7.20	6.04	10.60	8.75	15.21	11.50
Thailand	2.45	2.59	3.25	5.15	4.80	9.15	8.25	12.20	11.40
Others	1.00	1.01	2.15	5.10	4.20	8.95	6.25	11.85	8.95
Southeast Asia	26.82	27.60	33.55	55.70	47.59	76.50	61.25	105.11	85.00
Total	**75.34**	**79.03**	**93.65**	**137.62**	**119.21**	**182.61**	**148.61**	**237.46**	**191.65**

TABLE 4.2 (continued)

	1997	1998	2000	2004-I	2004-II	2008-I	2008-II	2012-I	2012-II
Percentage share									
Japan	56.40	54.28	51.13	45.38	45.64	39.76	40.23	36.80	37.51
South Korea	29.41	29.86	29.05	29.29	28.06	28.43	29.06	27.84	30.04
Northeast China	13.67	15.26	19.14	24.67	25.73	31.18	30.10	34.74	31.80
Russia	0.52	0.60	0.68	0.66	0.56	0.63	0.61	0.62	0.65
Northeast Asia	25.63	25.13	23.71	22.18	22.33	21.69	22.11	20.42	20.18
Hong Kong	49.78	46.53	42.61	36.87	39.78	33.16	35.23	30.77	32.22
Taiwan	29.03	27.94	26.12	25.70	28.56	25.56	28.90	24.81	27.44
South & East China	21.19	25.53	31.27	37.43	31.67	41.28	35.87	44.42	40.34
China Port Region	38.77	39.95	40.47	37.35	37.75	36.42	36.67	35.31	35.47
Singapore	52.65	54.71	50.52	43.00	45.60	34.64	37.96	34.63	37.06
Philippines	11.37	10.43	11.48	13.29	12.92	14.31	13.47	14.46	14.71
Indonesia	11.86	10.65	10.43	12.39	9.88	13.53	10.61	13.56	10.76
Malaysia	11.26	11.16	11.48	12.93	12.69	13.86	14.29	14.47	13.53
Thailand	9.13	9.38	9.69	9.25	10.09	11.96	13.47	11.61	13.41
Others	3.73	3.66	6.41	9.16	8.83	11.70	10.20	11.27	10.53
Southeast Asia	35.60	34.92	35.82	40.47	39.92	41.89	41.22	44.26	44.35
Total	**100.00**	**100.00**	**100.00**	**100.00**	**100.00**	**100.00**	**100.00**	**100.00**	**100.00**

I refers to the optimistic scenario; II refers to the pessimistic scenario.
Source: Ocean Shipping Consultants (1999) p. 197.

either economic scenario. Competing ports in Malaysia and Thailand are expected to experience a surge in throughput based on these forecasts, and it is this increase which is expected to dilute Singapore's dominance in Southeast Asia.

Patterns of transhipment

Feeder volumes have grown significantly since 1980, as not only has total containerized cargo trade increased by almost four times, but the incidence of transhipment[1] has more than doubled as the concept and practice of hubbing has developed around the world. It has been estimated that global feeder traffic increased eightfold from 1980 to1996 at an average rate of 14 per cent per annum (Drewry Shipping Consultants 1997, p. 6).

The development of major new transhipment-oriented ports at such places as Mina Raysut (Oman), Batam (Indonesia), Gioia Tauro (Italy) and Tanjung Pelepas (Malaysia) is clearly going to have (and in some cases is already having) a major influence on the patterns of cargo movements on many trade routes. When coupled with the inevitable upsizing of vessels on all routes, but especially on the arterial trades, operational and commercial factors[2] will also be working to promote a still greater incidence of relay traffic. Thus not only will the motivation to tranship be increasing, but so will the opportunity.

This points towards further increases in the transhipment incidence from its estimated 1996 level of 23 per cent to about 26 per cent in the future. This would mean that transhipping would make up a bigger percentage of container trade. With world container trade set to increase even further, although at somewhat lower rates than were seen in the first half of the 1990s, there is every reason to expect that transhipment activity and feeder cargo will continue to register good growth.

Table 4.3 projects the regional and global transhipment activity through to 2005, when the estimated worldwide port handling volume is forecast to be 73.6 million TEUs, and global transhipment incidence is forecast at 26.5 per cent. Average annual growth in transhipment/feeder activity is forecast at 7.6 per cent from 2000 to 2005. However this is well below the

TABLE 4.3
Forecast Global Transhipment by Region
(Thousand TEUs of Port Handling)

	1990	1995	1996	1997	1998	1999	2000	2005
Northern Europe	3,396	5,238	5,649	5,697	6,263	6,556	6,873	9,301
Southern Europe	1,656	2,970	3,654	4,306	4,910	5,478	6,038	8,469
Middle East	968	2,235	2,421	2,613	2,976	3,480	4,050	5,787
South Asia	409	703	974	994	1,019	1,029	1,076	2,147
Southeast Asia	3,876	9,455	10,615	11,680	12,958	14,353	15,804	24,325
Far East	4,343	7,724	8,288	8,865	9,522	10,171	10,809	14,048
North America	1,087	1,604	1,672	1,699	1,707	1,713	1,742	2,035
Carribean/Central America	222	781	982	1,355	1,775	2,092	2,405	3,181
South America	0	89	103	115	213	365	557	2,202
Oceania	44	81	88	95	102	109	117	162
Africa	225	1,177	1,216	1,286	1,382	1,474	1,565	1,988
World total	**16,183**	**31,886**	**35,471**	**38,975**	**42,827**	**46,820**	**51,034**	**73,645**

Note: Eastern Europe assumed to develop no meaningful transhipment volume.
Source: Drewry Shipping Consultants (1997) p. 6.

14 per cent long-term trend growth of container trade, and reflects the generally maturing market conditions which will characterize the container trade market as time progresses. Thus, the organic boost to relay volumes from greater cargo activity will start to slow down, while the rate at which the transhipment incidence rises can also be expected to reduce. Nevertheless, this still points to a transhipment market which will be characterized by increasing volume.

Southeast Asia is projected to remain the leading transhipment region in the world, and indeed ix expected to extend its lead over the nearest rival zone to some 10 million TEUs of port handling moves per annum by 2005. This is mainly due to the resumption of economic growth after the recovery from the recent currency crisis. In addition, with the joining of ASEAN by Vietnam, Cambodia and Myanmar, there are further markets to be developed which are expected to increase the container demand in the region. Singapore's share of this growth is expected to be eroded by other ports in this region, namely Laem Chabang, Port Klang and Tanjung Pelepas, although the industrialization of the next wave of Asian tigers (Myanmar, Cambodia and Laos) should provide opportunities for further transhipment business in the region.

Future proportion of transhipment

Table 4.4 assesses the development of regional shares of the global transhipment market, while Table 4.5 forecasts the regional incidence of transhipment.

Many important container ports, Singapore being one of them, owe 70 per cent or more of their recorded throughput volumes to transhipment traffic. What Singapore and such other ports as Algeciras, Colombo and Khor Fakkhan have in common is their strategic location. They are commonly located at or immediately adjacent to the arterial route around the world. Proximity to the East–West trade lanes is a primary requirement for a port to develop as a significant hub.

Away from the axial route, ports are restricted to purely regional transhipment activity at best, while in some areas of the world there is essentially no transhipment, either because exorbitant handling costs make relay practices uneconomic (such as Australia and much of South America), or because of inadequate port facilities or other commercial/operational factors (as is the case in West Africa).

While the two main canals (Panama and Suez) and the Straits of Gibraltar form three of four primary nodal points of the arterial route, it is the fourth, Singapore, which has virtually and single-handedly secured a place of absolute pre-eminence in transhipment for Southeast Asia. Not only is the region estimated to account for 30 per cent of global transhipment (compared with less than 14 per cent in 1980), more than 45 per cent of its total throughput is estimated to be generated by transhipment. Both these numbers are the highest in the world, as Tables 4.4 and 4.5 show.

Most areas are projected to experience continuing growth in their incidence of transhipment, with one or two notable exceptions. South Asia, for instance, is expected to see less transhipment in the short term due to a combination of

TABLE 4.4
Forecast Regional Share of Global Transhipment Market
(Percentage of Global Total)

	1990	1995	1996	1997	1998	1999	2000	2005
Northern Europe	21.0	16.4	15.9	15.3	14.6	14.0	13.5	12.6
Southern Europe	10.2	9.3	10.3	11.0	11.5	11.7	11.8	11.5
Middle East	6.0	7.0	6.8	6.7	6.9	7.4	7.9	7.9
South Asia	2.5	2.2	2.7	2.5	2.4	2.2	2.1	2.9
Southeast Asia	24.0	29.7	29.9	30.0	30.3	30.7	31.0	33.0
Far East	26.8	24.2	23.4	22.7	22.2	21.7	21.2	19.1
North America	6.7	5.0	4.7	4.4	4.0	3.7	3.4	2.8
Carribean/ Central America	1.4	2.4	2.8	3.5	4.1	4.5	4.7	4.3
South America	0.0	0.3	0.3	0.3	0.5	0.8	1.1	3.0
Oceania	0.3	0.3	0.2	0.2	0.2	0.2	0.2	0.2
Africa	1.1	3.2	2.9	3.3	3.2	3.1	3.1	2.7

Source: Drewry Shipping Consultants (1997) p. 117.

TABLE 4.5
Forecast Transhipment Incidence by Region
(Transhipment as Percentage of Total Regional Activity)

	1990	1995	1996	1997	1998	1999	2000	2005
Northern Europe	21.3	24.7	25.2	25.5	25.8	26	26.2	27.5
Southern Europe	25.5	28.5	31.0	33.0	34.0	35.0	36.0	40.0
Middle East	27.3	33.0	33.2	33.5	35.0	37.5	40.0	40.0
South Asia	23.1	21.9	26.2	24.0	22.0	20.0	19.0	25.0
Southeast Asia	40.3	44.8	45.7	46.0	46.2	46.5	46.7	48.0
Far East	19.0	18.8	18.6	18.4	18.2	18.0	17.8	16.8
North America	6.5	7.3	7.3	7.2	7.0	6.8	6.7	6.7
Carribean/ Central America	6.9	16.0	18.2	22.0	25.0	27.5	30.0	32.5
South America	0.0	2.4	2.6	2.8	5.0	7.5	10.0	22.5
Oceania	1.9	2.4	2.5	2.6	2.7	2.8	2.9	3.4
Africa	8.4	26.4	25.9	25.0	24.5	24.0	23.5	21.0
World total	**18.5**	**22.3**	**23.0**	**23.5**	**24.0**	**24.4**	**24.9**	**26.5**

Source: Drewry Shipping Consultants (1997) p. 117.

circumstances: capacity constraints in Colombo, additional competition from Middle East and, most important of all, port development and privatization in India which will promote more direct-call traffic. However, new transhipment terminals at Colombo and/or Galle (Sri Lanka) are subsequently expected to reverse this diminishing incidence of transhipment.

Due to the development of offshore transhipment facilities in the Caribbean region, which are expected to attract traffic away from the U.S. east coast ports due to both cost advantages and the possibility of circumventing Jones Act restrictions,[3] North America is expected to have a decline in its relay incidence. Potential capacity for transhipment business will also be affected by the expansion constraints in U.S. east coast ports.

The Far East zone is forecast to see further reduction in its transhipment incidence, partly due to the emergence of Chinese ports such as Shanghai, Yantian and Shekou as increasingly viable direct call options for mainline services, thus causing a consequent reduction in the transhipment requirement. With China expected to enjoy further economic and trade growths, it is expected that more ports will be developed for direct calls instead. Despite the lower incidence of transhipment, absolute transhipment activity and feeder traffic are still projected to rise substantially in future as a result of the above-average trade growth that China is expected to have.

The most dramatic increase in transhipment incidence is expected in South America where, from almost nothing in 1990, almost a quarter of port handling activity is expected to be attributed to relay traffic by 2005. One reason is the expected privatization of container terminals in Brazil, which will lead to the increased development of hub facilities. The introduction of international operators, along with their capital and expertise, will ultimately lead to massive increases in transhipment activity as terminal cost reductions alter the commercial equation between direct calls and feeding for ports in Southern Brazil, Argentina and Uruguay.

While the Caribbean Basin ports have already established a major presence in the global transhipment network, judging from the investment in new and expanded facilities, regional port operators are anticipating substantial growth in relay business. We have seen the inauguration of significant new transhipment terminals at Manzanillo (Panama) and Freeport (Bahamas) in recent years. The liberalization of trade with the main South American countries has radically altered cargo flow patterns and volumes in the region, which promises further substantial rises in transhipment flows.

Transhipment activity in Southeast Asia is also forecast to continue growing in line with the increasing propensity to deploying large mainline vessels to call at large ports, and to support the general growth in economic activity in the region, especially the markets of Vietnam, Cambodia and Myanmar. The region is expected to reach a figure in excess of 24 million TEUs per annum, from around 12 million TEUs in 1997. Despite the recent Asian crisis, the projections of increased volume in Table 4.3 forecast a growth rate of more than 10 per cent per annum of transhipment volume to the year 2005. Table 4.3 also shows that container demand is expected to grow at an average of at least 11 per cent per annum to the year 2012 even in the most pessimistic scenario, and demonstrates the requirement of another Port of Singapore in terms of capacity in this region.

Conclusion

It is predicted that further growth in container demand and transhipment around the world is expected in the future, regardless of which scenario is assumed. Continued growth in world trade, the trends towards deregulation and market liberalization, and the increased usage of containers in transporting cargo are the major factors underlying this expected growth. The trend by shipping lines to use larger vessels and call at lesser ports would be one important factor leading to an increase in transhipment. Southeast Asia is expected to capture most of the transhipment traffic.

Despite the continued concentration of transhipment business in this region, the forecasts will see the Port of Singapore lose market share to its regional competitors. Despite the increase expected in absolute volume, the developments of ports and economic growth of countries in the region are expected to be the main cause of this market share loss. Singapore currently enjoys high levels of efficiency, advanced technology, a wide range of services, extensive connectivity, high frequency of vessel calls and, in particular, the scale advantages relative to other smaller regional ports. However, to rely on the latest technology and investment in manpower to maintain its comparative advantage is no longer sufficient, as any port with resources can procure the latest equipment and, with privatization, staff can be trained easily by professional port operators. Since other ports in the region are already developing along these lines, it is likely that the growth in container trade and transhipment will be more diffused.

Notes

1. Transhipment incidence refers to the percentage of container trade that is transhipped.

2. Operational factors include increased growth in regional and world markets, while commercial factors refer to the upsizing of vessels and cost and time savings by not calling at every port.
3. The Jones Act requires that vessels used to transport cargo and passengers between U.S. ports be owned by U.S. citizens, built in U.S. shipyards and manned by U.S. citizen crews. This permits domestic shippers to levy rates substantially above comparable world prices, effecting a massive transfer from U.S. users of water transport users to U.S. maritime carriers.

References

Avery, Paul. *Strategies for Container Ports*, p. 15. London: IIR Publications Ltd., 2000.

Container International Yearbook (p. 91 Fig. 4.1).

Drewry Shipping Consultants. *Short sea container markets — the feeder and regional trade dynamo*. London: Drewry, 1997.

Investors Digest, "A preferred port of call", September 2000.

Ocean Shipping Consultants. *World Container Markets to 2012*, London: Ocean SC Ltd., 1999.

Port Authority of Thailand, *Newsletter* March 1999.

Straits Times, "Thailand may revive Kra canal project", 3 March 2001, A14.

5

The Seaport Model

In this chapter, we introduce a simple but effective decision-support toolkit to better understand the flow of containers (we have assumed twenty-foot equivalent containers) in the Asia–Pacific. This Seaport Model program can be used effectively to work alongside shippers and carriers who need to assess the value of direct shipment versus transhipment.

The Seaport Model program is targetted at the management of hub ports in the Asia Pacific region. The program enables an optimal shipping route to be found from a port of origin to a port of destination in the region. The program aims to enhance the ability to improve the sea transportation system with respect to the ports in the region.

By looking at how the optimal route changes when different decision criteria are used, this program can be used as a scenario-planning tool. The changes in the cost and lead time can also be compared and analysed between different optimal routes found, using different criteria. We can look at whether the increase in cost as a result of a shorter lead time is justifiable or worthwhile in order to achieve a faster shipment.

Building the program

The program is coded using Visual Basic 6 and can be run from a Windows 98/2000 platform which has Visual Basic capabilities.

A total of 15 ports in the Asia–Pacific region (see Table 5.1) are included and additional ports can still be added when necessary. These ports are chosen as they are either located in the capital of the country and/or they handle a significant volume of containers that justify their inclusion. Based on the decision criteria selected — cost, transit time, service frequency or a weighted average of these three criteria — the optimal route is determined using the shortest path algorithm, which can be found in any of the standard management science textbooks.

TABLE 5.1
List of Ports

Number	Port	Country	Port abbreviation
1	Singapore	Singapore	SNG
2	Bangkok	Thailand	BGK
3	Laem Chabang	Thailand	LCP
4	Ho Chi Minh City	Vietnam	HCM
5	Manila	Philippines	MAN
6	Jakarta (Tanjung Priok)	Indonesia	JAK
7	Hong Kong	China	HKG
8	Kaohsiung	Taiwan	KAO
9	Shanghai	China	SHG
10	Port Klang	Malaysia	PKL
11	Tanjung Pelepas	Malaysia	PTP
12	Tokyo	Japan	TOK
13	Bombay (Mumbai)	India	BOM
14	Colombo	Sri Lanka	COL
15	Pusan	South Korea	PUS

Data collection

Three types of data are collected for input into the program, namely cost, transit time and service frequency. Most of the cost data are obtained from the marketing department (Container Division) of the PSA. The transit time data are collected by obtaining the time taken from the port of origin to the port of destination by each of the four liner-operators: Maersk-Sealand, American President Lines, Hanjin Shipping and Uniglory Marine Corp. The final transit time for the program is then calculated by taking the average of the transit times taken by the four liner-operators. Service frequency data are obtained from the Containership Databank August 2000, again provided by courtesy of the PSA.

As the costs are based on different local currency denominations depending on the country in which the port is situated, the costs are converted into U.S. dollars to have an equal basis of comparison and analysis. Hence, cost is stated in terms of U.S. dollars per twenty-foot container (USD/TEU). The cost component is made up of the shipping freight cost plus the terminal handling charges (THC) for local and transhipment handling of the container. Local THC refers to the handling of containers for local consumption and import/export in the port of origin and port of destination. Transhipment THC refers to the handling of containers for transhipment. Transit time is stated in terms of the number of hours that a shipment takes to travel from the port of origin to the port of destination. Upon finding the optimal route, the number of hours will then be converted into the number of full-days by the program. Service frequency measures the number of shipments leaving the port of origin for the port of destination on a weekly basis.

Decision criteria

The first criterion is cost since it is often relevant in any business decision-making situation. More importantly, there is usually trade-off between the cost and lead time (in this case the transit time). In determining the optimal route, knowing the cost is essential to justify the use of a more costly but faster route. Furthermore, the change in costs due to a change in the lead time in terms of percentages can be analysed to provide a clearer picture and support the justification of using a more expensive route.

Transit time is the next criterion built into the program. Transit time is an important piece of information, as it is necessary to know how long a shipment takes from one port to another. With the emphasis on customer satisfaction nowadays, a company would not want cargo to be delivered late or too early.

Furthermore, if one can reduce the lead time relatively more than the subsequent increase in costs, taking a more expensive route can be justified .

Service frequency is the last criterion included in the program. Having this information will allow us to know the frequency of a particular service from one port to another. For instance, there are 495 services leaving Singapore to Hong Kong each week. Therefore, we can almost be sure that the probability of getting the cargo shipped from Singapore to Hong Kong on any day of the week is close to 1. It will also allow us to justify the decision of taking a more expensive route but with a higher service frequency between the ports. If the service frequency is low, then there may be a possibility of missing the service, which means delay and a longer lead time than expected.

Scenario analysis

The program can be used not only to determine the optimal route from one port to another, but also as a scenario planner to provide insight into the implications when a change in the weightage is placed on the criteria yielding the optimal route. We now illustrate this scenario-planning capability through some examples.

Mumbai to Tokyo

For instance, take a shipment from Bombay (Mumbai) in India to Tokyo in Japan, where we are interested to know the optimal route based on cost and time as well as a weighted average between these two criteria. The optimal routes, and the associated costs and lead time found by the program are shown in Table 5.2.

From Table 5.2, we can see that there is a difference of US$308 in terms of cost and 1.33 full-days if the criteria chosen are solely cost and time. This represents an increase of 35.76 per cent in costs as a result of a 6.79 per cent decrease in lead time. Hence, a reduction in the lead time does not really justify the use of a more expensive route. The next question to ask is whether there

TABLE 5.2

Optimal Route from Mumbai to Tokyo using Different Criteria

From Mumbai (Bombay) to Tokyo

Decision criteria (percent) (cost–time)	Optimal route	Cost (USD/TEV)	Time taken (Full-days)
(100, 0)	BOM–PKL–TOK	861.41	19.58
(0, 100)	BOM–PKL–TPP–KAO–TOK	1169.41	18.25
(90, 10)	BOM–PKL–TOK	861.41	19.58
(80, 20)	BOM–PKL–TOK	861.41	19.58
(70, 30)	BOM–PKL–TOK	861.41	19.58
(60, 40)	BOM–PKL–TOK	861.41	19.58
(50, 50)	BOM–PKL–TOK	861.41	19.58
(40, 60)	BOM–PKL–TOK	861.41	19.58
(30, 70)	BOM–SNG–TOK	909.41	19.00
(20, 80)	BOM–SNG–TOK	909.41	19.00
(10, 90)	BOM–SNG–TOK	909.41	19.00

are any other routes that can reduce the lead time without any significant increase in cost. To answer this, we choose an equal weightage with a subsequent 10 per cent increase and decrease for each cost ad time criterion respectively.

Based on a weighted average approach, we observe that the optimal route (BOM–PKL–TOK) remains the same as if we were to use only a single cost criterion. A new route becomes optimal when the weightage on cost is reduced to 30 per cent or the weightage on lead time is increased to 70 per cent. The new optimal route is now to tranship through Singapore instead of Port Klang before heading towards Tokyo. The cost and lead time difference for this new optimal route when compared to the previous optimal route is US$50 and 0.58 full-days. This represents a 5.57 per cent increase in the cost, which reduces the lead time by 2.96 per cent. In this instance, one has to make a decision whether to pay an additional US$50 for 19.00 instead of 19.58 full-days. However, if we were to compare this new optimal route against the optimal route obtained for the 100 per cent time criteria, in order to justify the use of this new optimal route, we note that a 22.23 per cent decrease in cost increases the lead time only by 4.11 per cent.

Thus, depending on which basis of comparison we are looking at, the use of an alternative route may or may not be justified. Through this program, we can also determine the weightage (criteria) that will change the optimal routing.

Manila to Shanghai

In this next example, we look at a shipment from Manila to Shanghai. The optimal routes will be determined based on each of the three criteria as well as a weightage average of the three criteria. The optimal routes and the associated costs and transit times are shown in Table 5.3.

From Table 5.3, we observe that three different optimal routes exist when evaluating each of the criteria and the weighted average of the criteria. If we focus on costs alone, then the optimal route is to ship direct from Manila to Shanghai. However, if based on service frequency only, the

FIGURE 5.1

Optimal Route from Mumbai to Tokyo via Port Klang
Based Purely on Cost Criteria

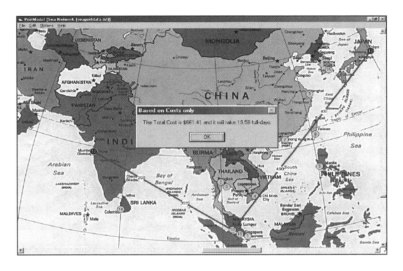

FIGURE 5.2

Optimal Route from Mumbai to Tokyo via Singapore
Based on 30:70 Cost–Time Ratio

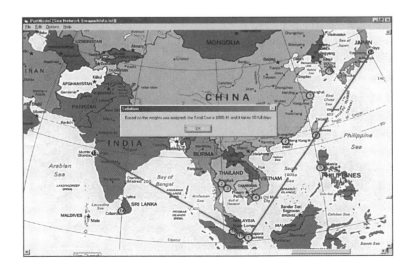

TABLE 5.3

Optimal Routing Based on Transit Times and Costs

From Manila to Shanghai

Decision criteria (per cent)	Optimal route (cost, time, frequency)	Cost (USD/TEV)	Time taken (Full-days)
(100, 0, 0)	MAN–SHG	498.11	14.67
(0, 100, 0)	MAN–KAO–HKG–SHG	742.11	6.21
(0, 0, 100)	MAN–HKG–SHG	667.11	9.42
(40, 30, 30)	MAN–HKG–SHG	667.11	9.42
(30, 40, 30)	MAN–KAO–HKG–SHG	742.11	6.21
(30, 30, 40)	MAN–HKG–SHG	667.11	9.42
(40, 40, 20)	MAN–KAO–HKG–SHG	742.11	6.21
(20, 40, 40)	MAN–KAO–HKG–SHG	742.11	6.21
(40, 20, 40)	MAN–HKG–SHG	667.11	9.42

optimal route will require the cargo to tranship in Hong Kong before heading for Shanghai. Furthermore, the transhipment point increases to two, going through Kaohsiung and Hong Kong, if the focus is on lead time only. For the weighted average approach, depending on the amount of weightage given to each of the criteria, two optimal routes are found, similar to the ones based on 100 per cent time and service-frequency criteria.

In choosing between the MAN–HKG–SHG and MAN–KAO–HK–SHG routes, we can compare the costs and the lead time. A glance at the costs and lead time would indicate that the latter is more worthwhile for shipping from Manila to Shanghai, since an additional amount of US$75 will reduce the lead time by 3.21 full days. Percentage wise, there is a 11.24 per cent increase in cost, which brings about a 34.08 per cent reduction in lead time. In any case, shipping direct from Manila to Shanghai is not a good choice, unless cost is a major issue or lead time is not as important as cost and two weeks of lead time is still acceptable.

FIGURE 5.3

Optimal Route from Manila to Shanghai Based on Cost Only

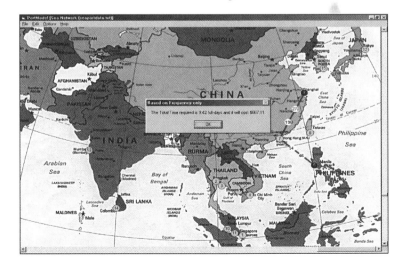

FIGURE 5.4

Optimal Route from Manila to Shanghai Based on Transit Time Only

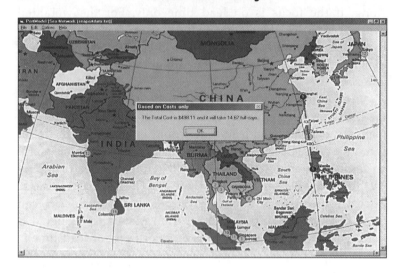

FIGURE 5.5

Optimal Route from Manila to Shanghai Based on Service Frequency

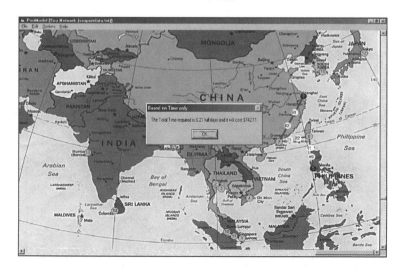

Conclusion

In all fairness, while the Seaport Model program has some economic and managerial contributions to make (through its capability to handle scenario-planning features and its ability to establish optimal routes), the limitations of such a decision-support-making instrument still exist. (For one, the data used to determine the optimal flow for container shipping are only as good as the user can provide.) In short, the model is still a static model. Ideally, a user would definitely prefer a dynamic model, one that is capable of interacting with changes in the environment. Despite this obvious shortcoming, we believe this model can still deliver value to the shipping industry, as a model for decision-making is better than having no model whatsoever. Moreover, this model-building has been approached with three rather than one criteria in mind, something that is currently lacking in industry. Analysing the results of such a model with the appropriate weights placed, one can then assess the importance of the 15 ports or so in their ascendancy to be hub ports.

6

Conclusion

This book has endeavoured to provide the reader with an updated overview of shipping development in Southeast Asia, positioned within the context of world shipping development. Broad objectives of port development targeted at countries within the region are provided, with a focus on containerized cargo. In Chapters 1 and 2, we have attempted to argue that current port development policies in Southeast Asia are largely driven by a rapidly changing business environment (globalization, deregulation and liberalization of port services among others), and technological advancements such as AGVs, EDI and IT. This then has naturally led to, *inter alia*, a broad discussion of strategies being adopted by shipping lines (including alliances and mergers), the operation of mega ports and the implications for port functions and inter-port competition in the region.

In this respect, we recognize that the competitive arena is always dynamic and one cannot predict to a hair's breadth the next stage or level of competition. For one, there is at present a "paradigm shift" towards using larger container post-Panamax ships. Recognising and embracing this shift in transport load, we were therefore at pains to update the reader on some port development policies and strategies adopted by ports in Southeast Asia — specifically those of the key ports of Singapore, Tanjung Pelepas in Peninsular Malaysia and Laem Chabang in Thailand. In particular, the Port of Tanjung Pelepas, within its proximity to

Singapore and major shipping lanes, offers a special case study in competitive port development strategy and competition posed against the more established hub port of Singapore. However, it is still too early in the game to predict, or even ascertain empirically, who will emerge as the ultimate winner in this numbers game. Clearly, as recent anecdotal evidence has shown, the Port of Tanjung Pelepas is gearing up for what appears to be a greater frontal assault on the Port of Singapore's container business.

Couched in this setting, we felt it instructive to provide another commentary on the status of the established and emerging regional ports. In this regard, the role, characteristics and critical success factors of hub ports are presented. While these might appear to be somewhat elemental in nature, they are nonetheless instrumental in garnering support for the need to have a multi-criteria simulation cum scenario-planner for ports and the shipping industry. In Chapter 3, we have seen how a hub port can diminish in status, a clear victim of the changing trade routes and supporting hinterland economies. In order to lend justice to the preceding statement we next offered in Chapter 4, a forecast of container volumes and patterns of transhipment. Past trends in world container volumes and forecasts of future world container volumes appear to suggest that container demand will remain robust for the next decade or so. This augurs well for the ports in this region and should serve as further fodder for more aggressive port development inclinations.

Finally, on this basis, we have offered to the reader a modest decision-support toolkit, the Seaport Model. This model uses the tri-criteria objectives of cost, lead times and service frequencies, all essential factors for hub ports. Based on secondary data provided by reliable industry inputs, we show that it is possible for two or more hub ports to exist in the region, depending on which of the three criteria are used. The upside for engaging in such a model is that ports and the shipping industry can, for a modest fee, employ a systematic approach to port planning and understanding of container flows through this region. We leave the reader — ports, port authorities and shippers — to decide if this is worth investing in.

Index

A

acquisitions
  maritime transport services 13
air cargo
  containerization 3
alliances
  development 27
  economies of scale 26
  maritime transport services 13
  shipping 15
  shipping conferences 14
ancillary services
  hub ports, importance in 58
approved shipping enterprise
  scheme
  Singapore 35
ASEAN
  container trade
    increase in demand 85
Asia
  container ports
    ranking 8
  container trade 19
    growth 80
  ports
    growth 9
    ranking 10
Asia-Europe
  container trade 19
Asia-Pacific ports
  Seaport Model program 92

Asian financial crisis
  impact 16
  Singapore, impact on 37
automation
  cargo handling 12

B

Brazil
  container terminals
    privatization 88
bridge services 30

C

capital costs
  container ships, servicing 26
cargo
  containerization
    growth 2, 3
    world traffic 4
cargo handling
  automation 12
cargo-information system
  Singapore 64
Caribbean
  transhipment facilities 87
charges
  container handling 70
Chinese ports
  emergence 87
competition
  advanced technology, role of 11

Hong Kong 61
Kaohsiung 67
ports, effects in 17, 24
Singapore 64
computerization
Seaport Model program 91
containers
charges, handling 70
larger, use of 102
Port Klang, handled by 40
container ports 7
demand, forecast on 77, 81, 82
ranking 8
transhipment traffic 85
upgrading 67
container ships
countries, according to 6
improvements 11
servicing, capital costs of 26
container trade
demand 103
growth 80, 89
transhipping
bigger percentage 83
container traffic
growth, factors in 76
container volumes
forecasts 76
assumptions 79
past trends 75
containerization 76
growth 1–3
productivity, raising of 11
seaborne 3
world traffic 4
costs
Seaport Model program 93
customs formalities
revision 13

D
door-to-door delivery 16
growth 29

E
East Asia
container port, demand 81, 82
electronic data interchange
(EDI) 31

F
forecasts
container ports, demand for 77,
78
East Asia 81, 82
global transhipment 84
transhipment incidence 87
transhipment market 86
foreign shipping services
Malaysia, dependence by 2
free commercial trade zones
hub ports 58

G
globalization
effects studied 19
ports, effect on 25

H
Hong Kong
competition 61
future development 60
future outlook 61
hub port 58
Port Development Board 60
port facilities 59
privatization 59
ship turnaround performance 59
transhipment 61
hub-and-spoke distribution
method

changes 55
hub ports 52
  capability 57
  characteristics 55
  competition, strategies for 67
  economies of scale 56
  efficiency 68
  environment, safe 58
  factors 57
  forecasts, regional 80
  free commercial trade zones 58
  future regional growth 69
  Hong Kong 58, 59
  human resources 68
  importance 53, 73
  Kaohsiung 65
  location 57
  management 91
  port infrastructure 67
  service reliability 68
  shipping services, simplifying
    56
  Singapore 62
  Tanjung Pelepas 69

I
Indonesia
  Koja Container Terminal 47
  port congestion 47
  Tanjung Priok 47
information technology
  computerized communication
    system 48
  impact 13
  inter-modalism, role in 31
  Kaohsiung, use in 66
  PortNet 63
  productivity, increase in 68
  TradeNet 63
  use 10
insurance companies

development, need for 49
inter-modalism 29, 31
  promotion 16
  Kaohsiung 66
  Tanjung Priok 47
  Thailand, development in 44

K
Kaohsiung 65
  competition 67
  container-rail system 66
  developments, recent 66
  future outlook 67
  information technology, use of
    66
  inter-modalism 66
Klang Port Authority 42
Kobe
  earthquake, recovery from 9
Koja Container Terminal 47
Kra Isthmus
  waterway project 73

L
Laem Chabang 43
  development 9
  future regional hub 72
logistics management
  recent trends 52
logistics planning
  hubbing, potential for 54

M
Malaysia
  seaborne trade 2
managers
  strategic location, rethinking
    of 52
Manila 45
  Shanghai, shipment to 96, 98, 99
  system 45

Manila International Container
    Terminal 47
manufacturing companies
    location 54
Marine Department of Hong
    Kong 59
maritime transport
    liberalization 16
    services 13
    Southeast Asia,
        dependence by 1
maritime transport services
    mergers and acquisitions 13
mergers
    maritime transport services 13
multinational corporations
    planned distribution
        hubbing 55
Mumbai
    Tokyo, shipment to 94
        optimal route 95

O

ocean-rail transport 30
operating practices
    improvements 12
optimal routes
    Manila to Shanghai 98, 99
        service frequency 100
        transit time basis 100
    Mumbai to Tokyo 95, 97

P

Pasir Gudang
    development 2
Philippines
    port authority 45
    water transport,
        dependence on 45
Philippines Port Authority 45
    ports, development of 46

planned distribution hubbing 54
ports
    Asian
        ranking 10
    competition, effects of 17
    container *see* container ports
    development policies 24
        future directions 48
        Manila 46
        Singapore 31, 32
        transhipment oriented 83
    ranking 9, 10
Port Klang 39
    future regional hub 71
    hub centre 41
    port authority 42
    transhipment 40
Port of Singapore Authority
    (PSA) 32
    Seaport Model program
        data collection 92
    ranking 9, 10
privatization
    Brazil
        container terminals 88

R

ranking
    ports 9, 10
routes
    Asia
        container trade 19

S

seaborne cargo
    containerization 3
Seaport Model program 91
    Asia-Pacific ports 92
    data collection 92
    decision criteria 93, 94
    development 91

scenario analysis 94
services
  development 49
ships
  container *see* container ships
  size, changes in 28
shippers
  port selection 69
shipping conferences
  alliances 14
shipping fleets 5
  country, by 7
shipping industry
  developments 25
shipping services
  changes, structural 11
  hub ports 56
Singapore
  approved shipping enterprise
    scheme 35
  cargo-information system 64
  competition 64
  contribution to economy 2
  developments, recent 63
  door-to-door services 35
  efficiency, improving 34
  future outlook 65
  government policy
    freight forwarding operations
      63
  hub port 62
  market share, loss of 89
  partnership with other
    countries 36
  planned distribution hub 63
  port 2
    development 31, 32, 48
  PortNet 34, 63
  social aspects, attention to 48
  strategies 33
  tax exemption 35

TradeNet 63
transhipment centre 86
transhipment, reliance on 32
Virtual Terminal contract 35
South America
  transhipment 88
Southeast Asia
  container trade, growth of 80
  maritime transport
    dependence 1
    promotion 7
  port development policies 24
  shipping
    overview 102
  shipping traffic, growth of 5
  transhipment 85
    growth 88
    Singapore's role 86
Subic Bay 47

T
Taiwan
  Kaohsiung 65
Tanjung Pelepas
  port, creation of 2
  Singapore, competition with 38,
    69
  transhipments 38
Tanjung Priok 47
tax exemption
  Singapore 35
technology
  improvements 25
  sea transport, effect on 25
  use 10
Thailand
  Kra Isthmus waterway
    project 73
  Laem Chabang 9, 43
  Port Authority of Thailand 43
transhipment

Chinese cargo 61
forecast 84
future proportion 85
growth 89
Hong Kong 61
hubbing 54
patterns 83
Port Klang 40
regional share, forecast on 86
Singapore 32, 62
    market share, loss of 89
South America 88
Southeast Asia 88
Tanjung Pelepas 38

volumes, rise in 75
transit time
    Seaport Model program 93
transport companies
    multi-modal development 30
transportation
    hubbing 53

V
Virtual Terminal contract 35

Y
Yemen
    Singapore, partnership with 37

The Authors

Mark Goh is Associate Professor at the National University of Singapore Business School and Director of Logistics Engineering at APL Logistics. He is also Associate Senior Fellow at ISEAS and Board Member of the Chartered Institute of Logistics and Transport (Singapore). His research focus is on supply chain management.

Chia Lin Sien is Associate Senior Fellow at ISEAS with many years of research activity on maritime transport.

Jose Lelis Tongzon is Associate Professor in Economics at the National University of Singapore with academic and industry experience in port and maritime economics.